T0193227

A word from the Author

There is a place of success and a place of failure. I have discovered the place of success with an invaluable price, this I have put into a golden vessel to serve you. Please, drink of it and be fulfilled. Do not allow the vessel to drop or its content, for they are my invaluable treasure. Drink, preserve and offer same to a true seeker of self-discovery success and fulfillment in life.

Other books by the Author:

-Fundamental Principles of Success and Fulfillment
-The Price for Greatness

Author's Contact

E-mail: <u>uffohonwe@yahoo.com</u>
          <u>hope4lifesolutions@gmail.com</u>
Facebook: <u>hope4lifefoundations@yahoo.com</u>

BRINGING OUT THE BEST IN YOU

THE BEST IS WHO YOU ARE

Uffoh Emmanuel Onweazu

 www.trafford.com

North America & international
toll-free: 1 888 232 4444 (USA & Canada)
fax: 812 355 4082

Dedication

To every man, people, community and nation that hungers after becoming the best.

Contents

Acknowlegdement

I owe the Almighty God unquestionable gratitude for the insight and inspiration for this work. This book became a reality despite all the oppositions and challenges because of His support.

I wish to express my honor to the General Overseer of the Redeemed Christian Church of God: Pastor E. A. Adeboye and all the people who have added positive value to my life. I am forever grateful to you all.

I want to acknowledge my loving and supportive wife Farida and our lovely children for their courage, God bless you all.

I specially thank all the members of The Redeemed Christian Church of God –Great House Orte Italy for all their support and encouragement.

Much appreciation goes also to all friends and well-wishers that have been there for me all throughout the time of this book.

Preface

The ability to discover the truth about your real personality is one factor that will definitely help you to find your place in life. It is the starting point of every man finding his footing in life and dealing with the problems of low self-esteem and inability to explore and maximize the potentials within and around him.

Each one of us represents the best. We are unique personalities as a result of the varying qualities and features that run through us. None of us is a misfit; there is a place that we clearly fit in excellently. This is the very reason you are the best.

Every time I am privileged to meet with people, one outstanding challenge I discovered is that lots of people find it difficult to accept the truth that they are the best. They are quick to point out the weakness and drawbacks in them and this blinds them of their uncommon strengths, abilities which they can capitalize on and make the very best of their life. In this way many have robed themselves their true personality. This is the basic reason most people are not living their real life.

This book **"BRINGING OUT THE BEST IN YOU"** was given birth as a solution to resolve this negative self-image. Actually, this book was the theme of a seminar. The demand to make a text became very necessary and as a result of the high demand of those in the seminar and those who in one way or the other have heard of this theme and the tremendous impact it has made in the lives of the participants.

This book is practically written so that it will help anyone discover himself and guide him to handle those limiting negative self-image and become the best in their chosen life endeavor.

Two things are necessary in getting the result from this book —the first is that you must believe that there is a best in you to be manifested and the second is for you to practically follow the various principles and strategies as you read them.

I hope that you will be inspired by this book and discover the truth that you are the best through this book as you follow the principles in it to make it a reality in your life. I wish you the best because you are the best.

Uffoh Emmanuel O

Introduction

One of the downside of life is to see yourself less than what you really worth. Unfortunately, this is one common drawback of most people. This state of less self-acceptance, undervalued and lack of self-recognition are factors that has handicapped so many people from maximizing their real potentials in life. I mean no one can bring out the best in him if in the very first instance he does not belief that there is a best in him.

Read my concept about all human and I strongly believe it will inspire you.

"There is a unique best in every one of us. This best is special, personal and very unique. You are the best, because you are a specially planned personality, designed, structured, built, commissioned and given a mandate to excel in every sphere of your life endeavor."

-Uffoh Emmanuel O

Each and every one of us is different from the next person, we all have differing features, abilities and talents that we can master, explore and prove ourselves as the best and thus accomplishing purposes in life.

Some features that clearly separate you from others for example includes:

   i. **Your finger print**
  ii. **Your vocal cord**

iii. **Your eye iris**
iv. **Special talents and abilities deposited inside you**

All of these features make you original, and thus this is for a purpose, which is to accomplish your divine and secular life that brings joy and fulfillment to you and those around you.

All men are created with an inner gem (abilities and talents) to make them successful. The fundamental task is the ability to discover your real purpose in life. This will help you in bringing out the best in you.

Discovering this truth about yourself will bring you to self-realization and a mindset to make the best of your life and not to live a life without meaning and purpose as we see in many around us.

The fundamental question one will be asking is how can we bring out this best that is in us?

In this book, I have written on some principles, twenty one (21) of them that anyone can adopt to bring out the best in them. Some of these principles include:

-Self-discovery and Realization
-Have a good opinion about yourself
-Never say you can't rather say you can
-Dwell in your place of joy and love
-Partner with people of like vision
-Learn from every mistake
-Never give up on your quest etc.

These principles are the very fundamentals, they are to be studied and as much as you can inculcate them into your life so that they become your lifestyle. This is the very key factor and method you can use to bring out the best in you.

Remember you are the best, because you are specially created for this purpose and your world is earnestly waiting for you to manifest this unique mandate that is in you.

Honestly it's your time to arise and shine. Bringing out the best is for everyone including you. I hope you will find this book useful in accomplishing you desire of bringing out the best in you.

Uffoh Emmanuel O

Chapter One

Self-Discovery and Realization

"Self-discovery is the power to unlock the door to your great wealth." –Uffoh Emmanuel O

The very purpose of life is to be able to discover who and what you are and be able to operate in that dimension. This is the only way that life can become meaningful and fulfilling to anyone.

You cannot live beyond the information you have about who and what you are created for. The understanding of this fundamental truth will make life much easier, enthusiastic and joyful for anyone. Read this:

"And God said; Let us make man in our image, after our likeness: and let them have dominion over the fish of the sea, and over the fowl of the air, and over the cattle, and over all the earth, and over every creeping thing that creepeth upon the earth. 27 So God created man in his own image, in the image of God created he him; male and female created he them. 28 And God blessed them, and God said unto them, be fruitful, and multiply, and replenish the earth, and subdue it: and have dominion over the fish of the sea, and over the fowl of the air, and over every living thing that moveth upon the earth."(KJV Genesis 1vs26-28)

"And the LORD shall make thee the head, and not the tail; and thou shalt be above only, and thou shalt not be beneath; if that thou hearken unto the commandments of the LORD thy God,

which I command thee this day, to observe and to do them" (KJV Deuteronomy 28vs13)

If you read through the above Biblical passages some information are clearly stated for you to know about yourself.

The first passage made emphasis that,

We are created:

-To be fruitful (i.e. being progressive in life)

-To be productive (i.e. being handy and useful to yourself and the world)

- Exploring every part of nature (i.e. creating something from nature)

-With a mandate to dominate our world and with no geographical limitation.

The second passage made emphasis that,

-We are to be the head and always be above only. What does this mean? It is being the best in our life endeavors.

This will ultimately become a reality as we apply our heart to work and acting with faith.

This information is highly vital if you will make the best of your life. You must accept the truth that you have inside you what it takes to be the best in your area of endeavor. This is the factor that will stir you up to do things the way that will bring you to the top.

Some people do not see themselves coming to this level in their lives. Why is this so? The reason is not far-fetched, some people are yet to discover who and what they are created to be and so they just flow along, allowing life to push them around. They are just like the shaft that allows the wind to carry it to wherever the wind directs.

The above passage reveals something interesting; that we are created in the image of God, after His very likeness, the implication of this is that we carry the genetic identity of God inside us. The creative potential is a unique ability that lies inside us. That is why I will emphatically say to you that:

Your destiny is in your hand

Your success or failure in life is a product of your lifestyle; if you chose to ignore your creator and live as one having liberty that has no restriction then you will end up like a speeding car without brake.

-Uffoh Emmanuel O.

How can you then discover yourself?

Let us see some things that you need pay attention to if you desire this self-discovery that will help you bring out the best of your life.

First you need discover that thing or activity that you do naturally well with ease and with passion. This is the very area that you can manifest and be the very best. There is no point trying to be what you are not made of, there is a purpose for your creativity that only you can fit and fulfill. There is no point trying to argue on this, the identity you carry is unique for that purpose that is why no other person carries the same identity like you. Discovering your unique purpose in life and fulfilling it is the ultimate satisfaction in life.

After discovering yourself these are the things you must do to realize this purpose.

Remember this:

Destiny discovered is destiny recovered

There are list of seven (7) important things you must do to make this a fulfilling one.

1. SET A GOAL TO BE ACHIEVED

Set a goal with a standard for yourself towards this vision or endeavor. You have to set that goal, let me call it vision. You must clearly and concisely state the vision. How do you do this? Simply by writing it boldly. Place a copy of it in a place where your eyes will always be in contact with it every day until you get it accomplished. There are huge benefits in writing your vision, let us see some of these benefits:

i. It keeps you on your toes that there is something important to be done for you to come to the place of the best.

ii. It keeps you away from distractions, because you are focus and on course towards accomplishing the said vision.

iii. You are able to cleverly eliminate every other thing that is not linked to the vision that will deny you the possibility of accomplishing it

iv. Every vision must have a time set for accomplishment. This will create a sense of urgency and with that consciousness move you to manage your time effectively to bring your desire to reality.

V. Writing your vision will help you to plan what it requires to achieve the vision.

2. WRITE OUT A STRATEGIC PLAN FOR THIS GOAL

Carefully plan a strategy that you intend using to turn your dream to reality. This is the second step that must be taken. Plans are very useful tool in achieving anything in this life. The plan is the road map in your journey to the shore of your dream. It is what guides you to the place of your dream; without it you are not likely to attain your vision.

3. LOOK FOR PEOPLE TO MENTOR YOU IN THE AREA

Search out carefully successful people in this sector and let them mentor you. This is very important; they will take you through the rigorous journey and reveal to you the mistakes they made and how you can overcome them. Importantly, they sometimes will give you the first network to advertise and sell your product or service in this career you have decided to take. They are your first point of leverage to become the best.

4. BE DETERMINED TO ACHIEVE THIS GOAL

Determination –persistence is the word, you will definitely face obstacles that will almost make you give up on your best. With determination you can break those walls of limitation and cross to the place of success. The best is in every man; this is the first significant truth. But to bring out this best in you demand real determination, without which becoming the best is not assured.

5. HUMAN RELATION

Human relation, this is very important if you lack good human relation it will negatively affect your desire to bring out the best in you. Of course most of your activity will involve dealing with people directly or indirectly. You will learn to relate, treat, and work with others in a manner that will earn you their trust, love and patronage. If any of these fails, you will definitely find it difficult than you can ever imagine.

6. BELIEVE IN YOURSELF AND YOUR GOAL

Self-belief and confidence are two very important characters you must demonstrate. Belief in yourself and your product or the service you are offering. It is what you belief in that you can do well and sell the product or service successfully.

7. REMAIN FOCUS

Stay focus and remain patient. These are two factors that will carry you through. If you lose focus you will miss your aim and if you lack patient you will be frustrated out of your place of purpose in life.

These seven factors are essentials for you to become your very best in life if you are able to inculcate them into your life and career.

ACTION POINTS AND WORKBOOK FOR CHAPTER ONE

1. Have you discovered your purpose?
2. What is the self-discovery about yourself?
3. Do you belief you can attain this purpose?
4. If your answer is YES, then proceed to the next point if NO go back to question 1 and discover your purpose.
5. Write out everything necessary for you to achieve your self-discovery.
6. Write out a step by step strategic plan to accomplish your self-discovery
7. You must set a time frame to turn your discovery to reality.
8. Do you need training and development to help you on this?
9. If your answer is yes, then go for the right training.

Take very strict action to make it happen and take absolute control of your self-discovery.

Chapter Two

Have A Good Opinion About Yourself

"Your opinion about yourself is your personal identity and not the opinion of others about you."

-Uffoh Emmanuel O.

A good opinion about yourself is a great factor that can help bring out the best in you. Say good things about yourself, you are not worthless or useless as most people confess when they come to cross roads in their lives. Let me show you something that will interest you.

"I will praise thee; for I am fearfully and wonderfully made: marvelous are thy works; and that my soul knoweth right well." (KJV Psalms 134vs14)

The above word is inspired confession of a man who went through various challenges and battles but recognizes the very personality that he is made of and he expressed it as written above.

Who do you think this quotation refers to? It is you. You are an amazement of God's creative power. This quality should always make you feel your uniqueness amongst other people.

There are some self belittling words that some people use on themselves, such as. "I am a failure in life"; "I cannot achieve success", "there is nothing about me that should make me be proud of myself."

You cannot have such downgrading mindset about yourself and expect to bring out the best in you when in the first place you do not see yourself as a best.

Words are powerful and you need to think and say good things about your life and whatever you are involve in. Do you know that a man cannot rise above his mental image? I simply put it this way:

A man's thought about himself is one factor that determines his altitude in life.

The Bible says:

"For as he thinketh in his heart, so is he..." (Proverbs 23vs7)

Let your opinion about yourself be positive, do not have a poor mentality, free yourself from the prison of low self profile. How do you see yourself? Do you see yourself as one with a great destiny, which will be a solution to the life of others around?

Self Confidence is the word, Yes with it you can get anywhere in life. You can create your life that will be without any form of limitation. Life has a way of making you feel inferior and people will sometimes do everything they can to make you feel inferior by talking you down and sometimes treat your ideas as nothing. But your personal opinion about yourself and your ideas counts and this self-confidence is the weapon to win in such times. Confidence brings you to real commitment of not giving up or allowing yourself to be displaced by others or situations of life.

In bringing out the best in you, in the endeavor you have chosen you will definitely require other elements to make this work such as—man, finance, structures etc. But if you lack that good opinion, I mean a convincing believe about yourself and the vision you are selling, it will be difficult for others to partner with you and no investors will be ready to trust their resources into your hands to accomplish your desire.

Without mincing words the best in you that you dream of accomplishing can become a reality by first having a convincing and enduring optimistic opinion about yourself and whatever you dare associate yourself with.

This is a serious issue; I have seen most people who have ended up becoming less than what they really worth as a result of some people's opinion about them and their vision in life. Do not give place to intimidation. This is one factor that can limit people in life. You are beyond intimidation, nothing can stop you accept yourself. There is great possibility potential inside you, and that is why I can boldly tell you that you can be what you want to be, you can be who you dream to be. Dream big of yourself, have a big mind that you can make it happen without being intimidated.

Hear this:

"Nothing is impossible for you to achieve if you can set your mind and life to get it achieved."

-Uffoh Emmanuel O.

One of my greatest discoveries in life is that life never gives you what you think you worth, but will give to you what you believe you worth and place a demand to have it with patience, persistence and with a positive attitude. These three qualities **patience, persistence and positive attitude** are of great importance. When other say you cannot be patient, stay persistence and continue with a positive attitude and it will amaze you that you can win above all odds that tend to stop you from delivering your best.

The abilities and talents that are inside you are to make you fit into the world and accomplish divine and secular purposes successfully. You have to see yourself in this perspective to actualize your desired best.

You are not cheap; you are invaluable, look deep into your life and see that there is greatness (abilities and talents) in you that others cannot offer better than you. Treat yourself with great respect; people will treat you the way you present yourself.

There are some atmospheres that negative opinion creates; you have to watch out for them and get rid of them. These are some of such:

1. **It tells you something is impossible even when it is possible.**
2. **It generates fear in you, instead of manifesting faith that turns desires to come to pass.**
3. **It makes you accept things the way they are even if they are negative and there is no future in it for you.**
4. **It forces you to rest in the present without taking a look into the future.**
5. **It makes you live a life of inferiority complex before and amongst other people.**
6. **It confines people to a point I call the comfort zone. This limits growth in life.**

This kind of thought about yourself must be changed for you to become what you have been made to be.

> **"Every man's destiny lies in their hands, it's in their thought and in their choice. What they belief about themselves and the actions they take in their lives."**

> **"Decision is all about what we belief and followed by the actions we take. Do yourself good by expressing a good opinion about yourself." –Uffoh Emmanuel O.**

Take a very serious time and think over the two statements above and allow them x-ray your entire life to know where you really belong.

ACTION POINTS AND WORKBOOK FOR CHAPTER TWO

Your opinion about yourself is very important. If you will excel in your personal or career life it highly borders on your opinion about yourself first. You will have to answer these questions sincerely and take the actions where necessary for you to manifest the best as desired.

1. What opinion do you hold about yourself, Positive or Negative?
2. If your opinion about yourself is positive you can proceed to the next action point but if it is negative you have to go back and read chapter two carefully to help you to make good opinion about yourself.
3. Write out seven to ten top positive opinions about yourself.
4. Write out the things if any you don't really like about yourself.
5. Measure up (3and4) and see if your positive opinion is more than the things you don't like about yourself.
6. Do you think you can deal with these negative sides?
7. If your answer is yes, then proceed by finding solutions to each of them.
8. If you think you can't deal with them, my advice is that you see a counsellor to help you on the issue.

Chapter Three

Never Say You Can't Rather Say You Can

To say you can't is creating barriers. But to say you can brings possibilities.

Never say you can't, rather say you can. You are mandated to be optimistic about your life. At creation you were made to be optimistic, not to think negative. If you are one of those who will never see possibility, there is no assurance that you will bring out the best in you.

One of the factors that affect your life is the confession of your faith, your confession about your life or things around you will cause them to yield success or failure.

The size of a challenge is not an indication that the challenge cannot be overcome. Those who allow the sight and sound of the challenge that confront them to say they cannot carry on with life and quit are not prepared in the first place to be successful.

If you can say you can, it is registered in your mind and everything in you will begin to work towards you being able to do that thing. This is the principle.

You can only do what you believe you can do and cannot do what you believe you can't do.

There are some Biblical concepts that can also be of help to you if you can work with them.

"I can do all things through Christ which strengtheneth me." KJV (Philippians 4 vs13)

The above quotation says we can do all things by virtue of Christ giving us the required strength.

"Therefore shall ye keep all the commandments which I command you this day, that ye may be strong, and go in and possess the land, whither ye go to possess it" KJV (Deuteronomy 11vs 8)

"Your ability to recognize godly principles and work by them delivers strength to you, to accomplish your desired goal."-Uffoh Emmanuel O.

In my secular and spiritual walk, I will boldly tell you that your ability to accomplish anything starts by your language. Success does not come with ease, you have to believe that you will make it happen and go out and give all it demand to see it come to reality.

One character I find out is that people walk away without first giving it a trial. They just allow life push them around from one point or place to another, simply because they cannot give life a little resistance. There is always an excuse just as there are reasons for everything. There is a saying that;

When there is a will, there will be a way.

Most people don't have the willingness to put up the little fight or the little push that will turn things around in their lives. Our world is created and mandated to operate under certain principles for good reasons. You must learn these principles and apply them to make the best of your life. For example, in physics there is a law that states that:

Every object in a state of rest will continue to be in that state of rest unless an external force is applied to it.

What this principle is saying is that things, situation, your life will remain the way they are unless you do something reasonable and positive about it. This is the only assured way to bring that defined positive change to your life.

The Bible declares a principle in this perspective, read this:

"Jesus said unto him, if thou canst believe, all things are possible to him that believeth." (KJV Mark 9vs23)

This is one principle that has worked for innumerable people and still works and will continue to work for those who believe and act on the principle.

Everything you need to make your life an accomplishing one is already in you. The only problem is that people find it difficult to believe and work with the relating principles and strategies that will bring their desires to reality.

We can be the person (i.e. who and what) we dream of and be where we desire to be in life. You are the only one that can create the limiting point for yourself.

I hope that you will stand today and bring a turning point in your life by accepting this undying truth that you can create unlimited life for yourself and rule your world as it is expected in the dominion mandate delivered to you at creation.

ACTION POINTS AND WORKBOOK
FOR CHAPTER THREE

You can't become what you do not believe the possibility. To say you can, creates a burning desire that is followed with an action to accomplish it.

1. The word "can" generate possibilities but can also generate impossibilities depending on the type of word.
2. What are things you see impossible for you? (Make a list of them).
3. Beside each of the listed impossibilities attach reason(s) why you think/believe it can't be attained.
4. Make a research finding out if there have been people with similar challenge and find out how they overcome them.
5. Apply the information you got step by step and see the result.

Bottom line

You are created with all you need to become whatever and whoever you desire to be in this life.

The task is for you to sincerely discover what you are called for and find what it will takes for you to reach that vision and you will be there.

Chapter Four

Dwell in Your Place of Joy and Love

"A career without joy and passion is likened to being in prison."-Uffoh Emmanuel O.

Life is uniquely beautiful when you find your place of joy and passion. This is a place where you are well fitted and you can do your endeavor with ease. Every one of us has his or her own place of joy and love.

The place I am referring to is the place of your purpose in life. We all cannot be Doctors, Engineers, Lawyers, and Architects Recording Artist and so on. The list is endless; some people have to do other life activities for the world to be a better place for each one of us.

You may be working a high class, well paid job but there is no love and satisfaction in you because it's not your place of passion that was not what you are called to be.

To bring out the best in you may sometimes demands that you study or get trained in the sector you find interest in and you know you are good in the sector based on some talents and abilities that you have relating to that field.

For instance, it will be a struggling effort for anyone having problems with numbers, figures and symbols to get into engineering activity.

Today, so many individuals in an attempt to please self or people around them decides to go and study or go for training that within them they know they are not wired for such. This is a case of self-deception. It is a complete waste of time, energy, finance and other valuable resources. The product of such deceptive lifestyle is regrets and frustration in the life of the individual.

If you can be true to yourself and integrate the time, energy and all other resources you wasted into that core area of your life that you are created for, you would have done excellently well at the end of the day.

We find, success, joy peace and fulfillment when we are engaged with the activity that we already discovered that we have some basic talents and abilities for.

Do not engage yourself into something because your friends are engaged into that activity. Be convinced, be realistic, cut off this sentiment thing and be your real self.

Whatever your interest is in life, you should have some self pride, do it well and you will be amazed that your originality will make you a need to other people. It is wrong for you to see yourself as ordinary or for you to see what you are doing as marking time.

Your gifts and abilities should be seen and taken precious; this is what will bring you to the place of honor and give you prosperity if you use it well. Let me show you something that will challenge your life and faith.

"A gift is as a precious stone in the eyes of him that hath it: whithersover it turneth, it propereth" (KJV Proverbs 17vs18)

Your gift is that thing that you know how to do well; it's likened to a precious stone that gives prosperity wherever it is taken to.

This is my question to you, have you discovered your gift? I mean your talent, how important do you take it if you have discovered it?

Whatever it is, you can do so much with it if you can appreciate it and explore every thing therein about that talent to make your life a joyful and fulfilling.

Let me inspire you more with some other words of inspirations, read this:

"A man's gift maketh room for him, and bringeth him before great men." (Proverbs18vs16)

The best in you can be harnessed to bring you before great personalities in life. That is why you must not look down on yourself or whatever you are doing.

"Whatsoever thy hand findeth to do, do it with thy might; for there is no work, nor device, nor knowledge, nor wisdom, in the grave, whither thou goest." (Ecclesiastes9vs10)

Whatever be the activity, be committed to it and put in everything in you and you will be the best in that sector. Success and fulfillment are the desire of every one of us wherever we find ourselves, but these does not come by default you must be in the right activity that you derive pleasure doing and be ready to give it what it demand for the expected success and fulfillment to be reached.

A square peg can best fit into a square hole, trying to put a square peg into a round hole will not work. The question is how can we avoid this problem of doing what we are not wired for?

It is by making a choice of career after a considerable deep thought on it. Making a choice of career in life is a long time decision and must be done carefully well. It is a life time thing and so must not be handled carelessly. You can adopt these steps.

Be realistic in choosing your life career

First and foremost, you have to be realistic. Be yourself, trying to be another person is an easy and simple way to fail in life. You are a unique personality, created to accomplish a unique purpose. If you try to imitate another person you will ultimately miss this purpose.

Let your choice be what you are passionate about

The second thing to do is to take a deep look into yourself and find out the thing or things that you enjoy doing and you do them well. This is a lead to your place of joy. Self-discovery is the first step to becoming successful in life.

Chose something that you belief in, something that you can flow with even when you face challenge in the career, you can stand behind it to defend it. All these factors will make your choice of career much easier to practice.

Find out what you require to accomplish your career

The third important thing to do is to find out what it will require to make this vision of yours a reality. In my little experience in life, one secret I discovered is that life will not deliver to you what you think you worth but will give you what you are ready to pay the price. So find out the price for the prize without this your desire will be a mere dream.

Make a winning plan on how to fulfill this desire of yours

The next thing to do is to draw up a winning strategic plan on how to make this goal a reality. Proper planning prevents poor performance, in whatever you are engaged in. This will help you check things out and know that there will not be any hitch by the time you launch into it fully.

Connect and network with other people

Another action that you must make is to look for successful individuals in this area and partner with them to help you out. This is call mentorship. This is the subject for the next chapter.

The last thing to do is to maintain winning character

You need to remain focus, committed, determined and be patient all through your path to the place of success that you desire.

ACTION POINTS AND WORKBOOK FOR CHAPTER FOUR

Finding your true path in life will make the complexities of life simple and easy. To be in a career because you want to please people will make you live a regrettable and empty life. Whatever is the case at moment you can take these action points and make the best of your life.

1. What is your current career or engagement life?
2. Sincerely answer "YES" or "NO". If you are happy with your career.
3. If your answer is NO write out why.
4. Write out what you would have wanted to choose as a career.
5. You can sure make a change to your true path in life if you honestly desire peace and fulfillment in life.
6. Start afresh, you are not a failure. You only made a mistake. Mistakes help us to know our limits and improve for the best.
7. Age is only a question of number. If your mindset is reach your place of you, you can get there if you dare push ahead.

Chapter Five

Partner With People of Like Vision

The people you partner with will make or mar your life.

Any vision without a good plan on how to turn it to reality may likely become a mere dream at the end of the day. One of the best strategic moves to turn ones vision to reality is to partner with people who have similar vision as yours and are making positive progress or have made notable success. This is what mentorship is all about.

Take time out and find someone or persons that you can relate with effectively, confide in and believe in their vision. If you can discover that person that positively influence your life and vision, then spend quality time in reading, studying and listening to his advice and ensure that you take action regarding what he teaches you. If you can strictly adhere to the various information and strategies you will definitely excel in the vision or career you have chosen to pursue.

Success is our paramount desires in whatever we are doing, but think about it if you want to succeed all by yourself it will be more tasking and demanding on you than when you decide to partner with someone or people with the common interest.

It is great wisdom to know that alone we can do but little but together we can do much. It's in agreement to the saying:

"Two good heads are better than one"

Partnership is for progress, progress is the product of good partnership.

Partnership is all about connecting and networking with other people, this means sharing information and ideas that will help bring out the best out of them. The ultimate purpose is to succeed easier and faster than when you are doing it alone.

Basic truth to keep in mind when partnering with others.

As we partner with other people for the purpose of achieving our visions in life there are some basic elements we have to bear in mind, this will help this idea.

Real partnership compliment individual's weakness

Partnership hides the weakness of each individual in the partnership because the strength of each compliments the weakness of the other fellow. True partnership is a strong strategy against individual limitations.

Trust is one strong element

Trust is the binding cord that will promote the purpose of any partnership, the day this cord is broken is the day the partnership starts dying. The level of trust you have for each other will create open mindedness that brings effective and efficient communication.

There will be times to compromise

I have to tell you that you must be ready to compromise in certain areas to make the partnership a success. Each one of us came from different background, culture, with differing philosophy about life, moral and civil. However, in the circle of partnership we have to learn to respect each other to accomplish the set goal.

Let the goal and purpose of partnership be specified

Partnership should have a specific vision and mission; these will help the partners to maintain focus and avoid distractions as they work towards achieving their goal.

The terms, Conditions and limitations must be specified

-Terms and condition of the partnership must be clearly discussed, agreed on and documented. This is very necessary; with this each partner will know their part of involvement and limit in the partnership.

The focus should be to make progress

-Partnership is built to make progress, if the partnership is not delivering this the best is to quit where there is no lasting solution to resolve the drawback.

Things to avoid that causes unhealthy partnership

-Keeping back important information that will advance the partnership on a positive direction. To hold back what your partner should know is a betrayal and believe me no partner will take it lightly if he finally discovers this act.

-Shifting responsibility can retard the goal of any partnership. You have to ensure that you do your part and do it well.

You cannot be in a partnership with a parasitic mindset and expect success. Partnership is a symbiotic relationship; we give our time, talents, skills and expertise to ensure that it is working well.

ACTION POINTS AND WORKBOOK FOR CHAPTER FIVE

You cannot under estimate the huge returns in partnership if it is done well. We cannot operate alone in this twenty first century and expect to accomplish so much.

A good team and delegation are factors that can help grow our personal, career and business life. It is worth cultivating.

1. Partners are people that will help you reach your goals in life easily and faster.
2. They are the very few that will stretch, challenge, encourage and leverage you to become successful.
3. You are not created to succeed alone, find the symbiotic individuals bring out the best in you by doing things the right manner that will help you get to the place of your dream in life.
4. Cut off all forms of sentiments, don't allow wasters and unprofitable folks rob you your great values and opportunities of becoming the best that you were created to be.
5. Partnership has rules that must be maintained for healthy relationship, enduring and progressive partnership.
6. Very important! If it's nothing working disengage from it before it ruin your person and career.
7. The best way to have a healthy partnership is to have a written and documented paper backing up the partnership.

Chapter Six

Learn From Every Mistake

Discovering or accepting your mistake is an opportunity to do it better.

No man is born perfect; we are all working towards perfecting areas of our lives that needs to be perfected. Mistake is one common phenomenon in life, which you cannot rule out the possibility in the life of people. This is simply because of the human nature.

In bringing out the best in us one of the issues we will need to contend with is the ability to avoid the same mistake over and over again due to careless or carefree attitude towards life. Each mistake we make in life is a lesson to take note not to allow the same to repeat itself. Very unfortunate many people will allow themselves to fall into the same mistake a second time or several times before they learn their lesson.

If you make the same mistake twice it is an indication that you have leant nothing useful in the previous mistake. Mistakes are actually teachers so learn something new from every mistake, otherwise it will repeat on you again. But here is a very important question.

Why you must not give up because you made mistake and fail?

Mistake is not a conclusion that you cannot achieve a thing but it is only to let you know that that is not the best way to go about that very thing to achieve it.

In my study on successful individuals; people we could say were the best in their endeavors. I have discovered that each one of them made mistake one time or the other in their lives before arriving to the place of the best. If this is the case, mistake should not make you give up on your dream or vision in life or in your quest to bring out the best in you.

Most times people back out on their way to success, they quit as a result of discouragement. This should not be the case, if you fail once as a result of your mistake, try again and again and you will make it. Those who fear of making mistake will end up as mediocre, since they refuse to trial something new.

In every mistake there are two lessons to learn and one important thing to do. The very first thing is to know the mistake, the second is to understand the consequences of that mistake and the third thing necessary is to learn from that mistake. These three things are highly important to make the best of your life.

For instance, when some people just discovered that things are not working well or they are not succeeding as they expect. Over and over again they keep trying and doing the same way. It is like a mathematical problem, if you are solving it with the wrong formula or equations you will definitely be getting the wrong answer. To get the right answer you have to solve the problem with the right formula or equation.

Another thing I discovered is that people are afraid that they will be ridiculed if they make mistake and so to avoid this experience they back out on doing something out of the box. Those who ridicule others that make mistake are ignorant of the truth that no man is born perfect, we all learn perfection through the events of life.

There is no point making ridicule of others, you are not better off. One time or the other you have made a mistake or will soon make one. If you can help others correct their mistake you have done well because this will definitely establish a good relation, who knows what this synergy will later develop into? I guess something good.

What to do to avoid mistakes?

"Anyone who has never made a mistake has never tried anything new" **-Albert Einstein**

We are human beings and every time we venture into new ground or into what we are not very familiar with there may be possibility of committing an error. But here is what is most important and that is to be much more careful not to do the same mistake a second time.

For us to avoid certain avoidable mistakes in life there are some practical steps we can adopt, such as these:

-Before doing anything you are not familiar, try to get a fore hand information or guidelines on how to do it.

-Don't rush into anything that you are not very sure of in the first place.

-Be patience in dealing with issues or things, take things step by step.

-Learn from those who have done what you are trying to do and get to know the possible mistakes that they suffered.

- Understand your strength and weak zones; mastering your strength and improving on your weak zone.

These are some practical approaches we can adopt to avoid certain mistakes in life both in our personal and professional life.

The truth you must always remember about mistakes

It's of utmost importance that we all know these truths about mistakes. The understanding of these will help every one of us to get out from the discouragement and self-pity that most people often suffer after they discovered that they have made a mistake.

-You are different from your mistake

There is a common error I have seen among many people and this is making themselves their mistakes. Oftentimes people when they make a mistake they are weighed down more confused and they wear this look that almost everyone they meet on their way will definitely know that something has gone wrong somewhere. This is a very wrong way to approach life mistakes. Alright! You have made a mistake but you are not the mistake, you don't have to put it on as a tag on your face that everyone that sees you will have to comment on. The worst effect here is that most people that are loud about your mistake are not better off; some of them have more mistakes and failure attributed to them.

Here is the way to go about it. Have you made a mistake? Yes agreed but is part of life. It is one of the things that we go through that leads us to perfection. Those who speak theoretically have nothing to offer you in times like this. Take off the defeated look off you and put on the winners look that separates you from your mistake and move on with your life.

With this new atmosphere around you go give it another try and you will see yourself making the best in that same thing that seem a no go area.

-You are to learn something in every mistake

Every day is a class room where we learn through events of life. In every mistake that you go through, there is some important to learn in it. If you don't learn anything from your mistake, then it is a failure. But learning something from it makes it an experience.

-At the edge of the mistake lies your success

Every mistake takes us closer to our desired success. Your success lies at the edge of that so call mistake that wants you to give it up. If you can stay and push harder, you will see yourself breaking the ice.

-Yours is not the worst

To think you made the worst mistake is to be hard on yourself. All men has their own mistake but you never know until they sit you down and tell you how many times they failed before arriving to the place of success that you celebrate with them.

-A mistake, why did it happen?

Normally, when we make a mistake we scream, jump and make noise but how many of us are careful in asking why it happened? This is the secret of winning over that mistake. You must answer this question correctly before you make the next move that will lead you to your success.

-Take responsibility of your mistake

Refusing to take responsibility is destructive. When there is a mistake it is not a time to a portion blame and start finding fault on people. This is the place most people miss it. You must take responsibility; if you can take responsibility then you can control the situation.

-Look beyond the mistake and see your success

Always focus on your success don't allow the sights and sounds of the mistake distract you from your desire. Look beyond and above the present circumstances and move on.

-Mistake is one product of fear

A mistake sometimes occurs as a result of fear on our part. The moment you have doubt and fear start generating in you go and do something there is no assurance that you are not likely to make a mistake. The first thing to do is to conquer your fear first before proceeding in what you intend doing.

ACTION POINTS AND WORKBOOK FOR CHAPTER SIX

Mistakes are errors that occur in life, for example when we do things the wrong way or we say somethings that is inappropriate to others. It is unfortunately a part of man, and we are all working towards perfecting areas in our lives where we discover errors.

One important truth you must take as a rule in your life is that mistake is not a conclusion that you can never do it the right way. It should not be taken that you have failed. It becomes a failure if you refuse to do something more reasonable to correct the mistake.

You will need to check out these questions and actions to help you deal with the issues regarding mistakes and how to resolve them.

1. Have you ever made a mistake?
2. Have you made the same mistake twice or more times?
3. How did you feel about this mistake the second time?
4. Have you been able to resolve the mistake?
5. Did this mistake cost you something or is costing you already?
6. The only way to move forward in life is to resolve to correct this mistakes otherwise you will remain retarded and unfulfilled.
7. Every mistake you do should not be seen as a permanent condition but should be taken as a form of practice that will lead you to a perfect success.

Chapter Seven

Never Give Up On Yourself or Your Quest!

To give up is defeat but persistence brings winning

Life can be demanding sometimes, and trying to strike the required balance in all areas of life becomes complicated and difficult as a result of reasons you cannot personally handle at the moment in question. The person that finds it difficult to make this balance should not kill himself if for the moment things are not working well.

To give up is saying you have lost hope for living. The situation maybe devastating however, you have to understand that the journey of life is in phases, and every phase has what is peculiar to it. This is the open secret most people have not discovered; this truth about times and season. Nothing is permanent save change; because change is constant the state of things will change with your little persistence.

It is not over with you just take faith and courage and face the situation, with God on your side you will win. Read these statements.

"Watch ye, stand fast in faith, quit you like men, be strong." KJV (1Crithians16vs13)

Stand up and face the situation with everything left in you backing it up with faith and be very courageous and you will see the barriers giving way. You don't expect to be the best without conquering the challenges that every best faces. God never promised us that the road will always be smooth all through but he did promise us a future and an expected end. See this in this amazing scripture.

"For I know the thoughts that I think toward you, saith the LORD, thoughts of peace, and not of evil, to give you an expected end." KJV (Jeremiah 29vs11)

This is a sure word that should stir up your faith that the current situation is not the final story about you.

Life is a battle and a battle of hope, those who quit when the battle is tough are not qualified to put on the winners medal. You are not qualified for the prize unless you have rightfully paid the true price.

Have you lost your business? or your career is hitting the rock perhaps you have lost your job, the only source of income for you and the family or too bad you have lost someone too dear to you. The situation or challenge has already happened. This is one truth you have to settle in you but above all you have to clearly know that this is a phase of life and move on. To stay in the situation or challenge is to be buried with it but to rise up and look beyond the current state of things is a step that can make you win.

Life doesn't give to you what you thought you are qualified for but will delivered to you exactly what you are willing to pay the price to have. Our world is governed by principles and these principles are universal. Working with these principles will help you in bring out the best and objecting to them will bring failure.

Success and failure are two opposing states. You will make a choice on the state you want to belong. Refusing to give up on your desire to be the best will no doubt deliver to you success. Those who desire success as their only option in life will never give up in their quest to bring out the best in them until they get it achieved.

"I am too big to cry and too badly hurt to laugh, yet I persevere." -Abraham Lincoln

This is one man who refused to give up on his dream. He resolved to keep the fight until he attained his desire. Never give up on whatever you believe in, if you fall rise and standup, if you are broken down, collect together the broken pieces mend it and keep going until you get to the shore of your journey.

It is a competitive world with not too many opportunities and there are multitudes fighting for this not too many opportunities. Make that last move and you will see that you have something in you that will enable you to reach your desired goal. When the journey of life becomes dark like the night time wait for the daylight, when you are tired and weary rest and move on. This is the spirit and the way to get your quest attained.

Your success or failure in life starts in the mind and this imagination is what you speak out and that finally determines the action you manifest. If you believe you can do it then speak that to yourself and move on and you will see yourself accomplishing that thing that looks seemly impossible. Read this:

"Jesus said unto him, if thou canst believe, all things are possible to him that believeth." KJV (Mark 9vs23)

"I can do all things through Christ which strengtheneth me." KJV (Phillipians4vs13)

You can draw inspiration from this passage of the Bible. You can be whoever and whatever you desire.

In today's world you see so many people giving up on themselves and their vision due to some irrelevant reasons. Some will say that age is not on their side and so they give up without trying. Very unfortunate, age is a question of number, you have to try and see how far your strength can take you before you conclude that you cannot.

Another individual will say it is very difficult, in the very first place who ever told you that life is a bed of roses or that to make success in life is very easy. If is so easy everybody would have been successful.

Success is for those who desire to separate themselves from the large majority by refusing to give up.

Some other people will say that they do not have what it takes to achieve what others are achieving. This is a typical excuse for those who are lazy and it is this slothful attitude that has left them among the ordinary. If you feel or believe you do not have what others that are achieving success possesses go and learn from them. True success is not magic, it's all about applying the same principles, strategies and steps that the successful applied and you will see it a reality in your life.

Never give up on yourself or your quest; nothing can stop an individual from turning his dreams and aspirations to reality like excuse. I personally see this life as a market place and the world will sell to you the products or services that are equivalent to the value of your money. Nobody wants to loose in the trading table, even when there is a discount the owner of the product or service will still sell to make profit. This is the reality of life and failure to accept this truth will doom an individual.

So don't give up, pay the price and be the winner you have ever dream to be in this life and you will be a role model that others will want to follow. If this is your dream life then it's time to move and don't give up on yourself. I strongly assure you that you can make it to the place of the best if you can let go the self-pity and excuse and challenge yourself to be the best.

Read about a man who was faced with so much challenges but he refused to give up until he got his dream achieved, in one of his writing he wrote this inspired word. I hope you will be inspired by this word.

"But we have this treasure in earthen vessels, that the excellency of the power may be of God, and not of us. 8 We are troubled on every side, yet not distressed; we are perplexed, but not in despair; 9 Persecuted, but not forsaken; cast down, but not destroyed;" KJV (2Corithians 4vs 7-9)

ACTION POINTS AND WORKBOOK FOR CHAPTER SEVEN

The best don't quit but stay on course until they prove themselves as the best. Life does not give to you what you think you are qualified for but will deliver to you exactly what you are ready to pay the price to have. Our world is governed by principles, and these principles are universal. There areas in life you must not give up and some of them include:

1. Never give up on yourself, whatever and who you conceive to be can be possible if only you can stay on course and refuse to give up.

2. Your vision, you must not give up on your vision in life, whatever the challenge may be if you conceive the vision then you must do everything you can to make it happen.

3. Your partners, your partners have role to play in your success, as long as they will remain in the vision with you, you will not give up on them but rather look out ways to call them to order if they are losing focus.

4. Never give up as a result of challenge, on your way to bringing out the best in you. You can't run away from possible challenges, it is a normal phenomenon, you must overcome that challenge. In such time, most important is your attitude, you have to be positive minded by looking beyond the challenge but focus on your desire success.

Chapter Eight

Be Focused, Cut Off All Distractions

**Without focus there is no assurance you
will arrive at the shore of your dream.**

We cannot arrive at our destined place of success and fulfillment if we allow ourselves to be distracted. It is important to know that without focus we cannot bring out the best in us, nor can we give our best in whatever we are called to do.

Focus is a thing of the mind and eyes; it is a state of conditioning your mind and eyes to the issues or agenda that matters most in your life that will add positive value to your personal and career life.

In our natural world there are so many distracting elements that contend with us. Such as -environment, man, personal habit, socio cultural activities etc. If we do not carefully watch out we will be driven off our dream track and may never be able to find our way back. This is what distractions is aim at doing to their victims.

In order to remain focus in whatever you have decided to pursue in life, it will require being disciplined. A self-controlled lifestyle is the secret to achieve this.

**You must know where you are going to in
life for you not to end anywhere in life.**

Life is not only complex but complicated and sensitive; you must remain focus to deal with it and get rid of all those elements that tend to limit you from reaching your desired goal. You must know where you are going to in life for you not to end anywhere in life.

Let us consider some of these elements of distraction.

Environment

The world is a center of influence. Influence brings change and change can be positive or negative. The environment you find yourself will try to influence you with her peculiar factors -positive and negative.

It is focus and disciplines that will enable you make the right choice that will enhance your success.

You don't accept every philosophy, culture and ideology on the ground that everybody is doing it, no! If it is going to hinder you from making the best of your life don't subscribe to it. One of the beauties of life is that we all without exception are given the power of choice.

This power of choice gives you the ability to choose your lifestyle, the circle you want to belong to, who and what you want to be address as. The fact that the environments you find yourself are full of drunks, gangsters, and people with questionable character does not mean you cannot make the positive difference. One Bible passage puts it this way.

"Wherefore come out from among them, and be ye separate, saith the Lord..." KJV (2Corinthians 6vs17)

You have to choose from the things and the persons in the environment that will positively add value to you and the rest you do away with them so that they do not distract you from your dream.

It may not be so easy to get this done, note carefully this is one decision you must make if you really desire to move your life from being ordinary to excellency. This is one great action you must be willing to take at every point in your life to move you to the next level of your life that will definitely help you in remaining focus to your goals and visions in life.

Personal Habits

Habits are some actions that individual do repeatedly, they are those actions carried out on regular basis consciously or unconsciously. These habits may be good or bad habits. If they are adding value to your life and career we can classify them as good otherwise they are bad ones that need to be eliminated.

Take for examples; if you are known as a person that is always late to meetings, you always procrastinate in doing your responsibility, you are not straight forward in your dealings with people. All these are typical examples of bad habit and such cannot move your personal or career life forward.

Lateness to events and procrastination are clear indication that the individual is not a good time manager. One of the simplest ways to fail in life is for an individual not to know the value of his time each day or not being able to convert his time to a profitable result.

Most of life activities will link us to dealing with others directly or indirectly. It is a great drawback on the part of anyone who is not straight forward. If people find out that you do not have a character you will loss the best factor that people look out for before they do things with you or entrust something to your care.

As much as we desire to make the very best of our lives it demands us maintaining good and quality personal habits that will promote our desire of becoming the best.

Social lifestyle

Good social lifestyle is profitable, but when you allow yourself to lose focus on what should matter most to you as a result of social activities then you have missed the mark. It should be business before pleasure and not pleasure before business. It is not normal for you to spend most of your valuable time in watching TV programs, going from one club to the other only to hear music or watch people dance. This is time, energy and financial resource that are being consumed with no reward. In my humble and honest opinion you can convert these times, energy and finance to your life interest and see how the result will become.

Socializing is good and encouraged but it's not wise or reasonable to allow yourself to be carried away with things that will not add in any way to your progress.

There should be a bold line drawn to clearly differentiate social time and work time. This is a sure way to remain focus.

Man

People can be a big source of distraction mosttimes. No man is indeed an island, and because of lack of man's imperfection we want to open our doors to allow people into our lives. Unfortunately, this gives access to even those who will limit us as a result of their bad influence and bad lifestyle.

Your success comes first above other things. If you find anything that will hinder this purpose, then it is a hindrance and must be eliminated if you will make it to success.

When you are focus in life it makes your life meaningful, purposeful and above all there is a sense of honor that you feel that at the end you would have accomplished something significant.

I urge you to remain focus and do all within your power to cut off everything that tends to risk your success plans and goals. This is the only assured hope of your becoming the best.

ACTION POINTS AND WORKBOOK FOR CHAPTER EIGHT

One of the foremost challenging or contending factors that faces individuals in the quest to be the best is the issue of distraction. There are so many distracting elements all around us. We have to take time to get them off our path before they hinder or truncate our vision of making prove of manifesting the best.

You have read out the main chapter, here are some basically action points.

1. Environment distractions, Most often people will come up with the excuse that there environment has caused their drawbacks. It is an excuse that is not acceptable since in the same environment we can find people setting the pace in their areas of interest. In my opinion it's more of choice, our environment no doubt has some influence but we have a choice not to allow ourselves to be negatively influenced.

2. Personal Habits, We are who and what we are today as a result of our habits yesterday. If the habits of yesterday has honestly led you to the very place of the best then continue. However, if it has not given you a view of becoming the best there is a need for absolute change of your habits.

3. Social Lifestyle, The word is a place of interaction; we are not created to operate separately. Our social life can help promote our decision to bringing out the best in us. It can also hinder people from being the best if that social lifestyle is not helpful to us. To live to belong most times is a sentimental decision that brings failure and destruction of your real purpose in life. Think about this and watch your social life.

4. Man: one of the greatest forms of distraction is man. Our friends, family members etc. In as much as you want to relate and allow people into your life it is very important that you still check out if these people are adding value into your life or they are they obstructing you from accomplishing your desire to be the best.

5. Other people's business, Learn to mind your business one of the mistake most people make in life is completely giving themselves to other people's business and forget about their own business. Don't get involved and carried away that your own business will begin to suffer loss.

Chapter Nine

Invest and Manage Your Time

Time is a divine gift, which we can invest to acquire or accomplish excellent purposes in life.

We live in an era where the value for time is highly very important yet most people have not realized how the mismanagement of their time has been their major drawback in life.

Time is a free gift to every living soul but with a purpose. Each day we wake up twenty four hours is deposited into our life bank, this is to acquire or accomplish purposes that will make our lives meaningful and satisfying.

To bring out the best in us demand our ability to invest and manage our time effectively without this you cannot be the best as you expect.

Our geographical location, background, status are no drawback to this gift of time that is deposited into one's life each day. Each one of us must be committed to explore this gift to come to successful and fulfilling platform in our personal and career life. Read this concerning time and you will be inspired.

"To every thing there is a season, and a time to every purpose under the heaven: 2 A time to be born, and a time to die; a time to plant, and a time to pluck up that which is planted; 3 A time to kill, and a time to heal; a time to break down, and a time to build up; 4 A time to weep, and a time to laugh; a time to mourn, and a

time to dance; 5 A time to cast away stones, and a time to gather stones together; a time to embrace, and a time to refrain from embracing; 6 A time to get, and a time to lose; a time to keep, and a time to cast away; 7 A time to rend, and a time to sew; a time to keep silence, and a time to speak; 8 A time to love, and a time to hate; a time of war, and a time of peace. 9 What profit hath he that worketh in that wherein he laboureth?" KJV (Ecclesiastes 3 vs1-10)

What the above is explaining is simply that everything in this life revolves round the concept of time. If you will make the best of your life it borders on your ability to manage your time effectively well.

We are all equipped with knowledge, **talents, ideas and acquired skills** that we can all transform into success and wealth but the major challenges that is confronting most people is their inability to maximally use their time to do what need to be done to convert these resources to a profitable outcome.

Let me show you sometime amazing. It's all about a very small creature but whose lifestyle is worth learning. The ant is very small in size yet has a value for time management. We can take a lesson from the ant as we read this about them.

"Go to the ant, thou sluggard; consider her ways, and be wise: 7 Which having no guide, overseer, or ruler, 8 Provideth her meat in the summer, and gathereth her food in the harvest. 9 How long wilt thou sleep, O sluggard? when wilt thou arise out of thy sleep? 10 Yet a little sleep, a little slumber, a little folding of the hands to sleep: 11 So shall thy poverty come as one that travelleth, and thy want as an armed man." KJV (Proverbs 6vs6-11)

The ants cleverly understood that at summer they have to gather all the food they will need during the wet season when it will be very difficult for them to gather food. Here the ants demonstrated a high sense of wisdom in managing their time to do the right thing in the right time. Most people will expect someone to push them, follow them every step before they will use their time to their benefit.

The question is how many people are utilizing their time profitably? If we will be sincere to ourselves not more than thirty percent of humanity are using or truly investing and managing their time effectively.

To bring out the best in us our time ought to be invested into relevant areas or sectors of our lives for a meaningful life that others will desire. Your live on the face of the earth is not for ever, there is a time frame. A consciousness of this truth will help you to face life with a specific vision or goal that you should have attained at the end of life.

How then can we invest our time for profit?

-Developing ourselves in activities we are doing or we intend to do.

-In exchange of things that will add value to our lives now or in future.

-For profitable ventures that will earn us economic resources to meet our physical needs in life.

-By engaging in other activities that will help develop us spiritually.

-Investing it in developing other people by offering services that will benefit them —academically, career and spiritual wise.

The above five areas are highly vital in becoming the best. If you cannot do these things then you do not have value for time. The value you place on time is equitable to the value of your life. Research has confirmed that time management is one factor that has defined individuals.

The moment you are able to organize your time your life will become more organized and meaningful. This is because you will plan and live each day with a goal oriented mindset.

Some effective ways to manage our time

There are some ways we can employ to effectively manage our time to get a more organized life. Remember that each day has twenty four hours and this time has to be effectively distributed to get a maximum use of it.

1. Get time management/scheduling tool, examples include: Mini diary, electronics devices such as phones, tablets, PC'S etc.
2. Make a "**TO DO LIST**" this is where you write out all you intend to accomplish in this form as it suits you.
    -Daily
    -Weekly
    -Monthly
    -Yearly

You can always make a review on your "To do list".

3. Beside each of the proposed "To do list" attach the date, time, place and add a brief description of what your focus will be.
4. More effective way is to download some application where you can enter everything as in (3) and have an alarm set to it as a reminder.
5. Make a commitment to this process and follow it and you can be sure that your time will be very rewarding each day.

Time is so precious and cannot be played with because it is brief. The quality of your life can change by the quality of time you put into it. Look for things that waste your time and eliminate them, stay far away from those friends that have no value for time.

Successful and great men and women has some unique characters or habits that are common to them and in my close research one remarkable character that they all identified with is the concept of time management. They agreed and belief that the concept of time management is one strong element that assures success in life.

Everything in life has a life span; nothing stays forever here on earth. If this is the case we must use our time only on things that will deliver positive results and profit to us.

It's surprising that some people are yet to be conscious of the value and importance of time and they live their lives as though there is a duplicate somewhere that they can come back with once their time is up here on the face of the earth.

Everything you want to achieve can be achieved, it only require the element of time. If you can give it time and patience you will see yourself turning your dreams to accomplishments. Sometimes you feel you can't make something happen but all you need is time and you will turn what seem impossible to possible.

Thomas Edison was told his dream to make the electric bulb won't work. He only asked for time, with more time to carry out the experiments, he was able to make his dream a reality.

What do you want to make out of this life? Whatever it is you can do it if you give your time and self to it like Thomas Edison did.

ACTION POINTS AND WORKBOOK FOR CHAPTER NINE

Time is an essential factor in our life, it's so important that if we will excel in life it will depend on how we manage our time. Most people are yet to understand this truth about time and that our lives revolve round the concept of time.

These are the action point to make best of your time.

1. Carefully monitor your life activities to discover if you have been maximizing your time to your benefit.
2. Write out and eliminate all those activities that do not add value to your life.
3. Reorganize your life by reorganizing your activities with specific time attached to each of them.
4. Use time management tools to properly effect this change.
5. Make a commitment to yourself to follow up on these action points and your time will be very rewarding each day.

Chapter Ten

Learn To Tolerate Others

People have their weakness and strength, which manifests as they interact with others. But with tolerance you can flow with all people.

-Uffoh Emmanuel O.

There is a best in each one of us, but this best does not automatically begin to manifest until it is discovered, patiently nurtured, packaged and properly delivered.

Most times people need to be guided for them to bring out this best; this is where the need to tolerate others becomes very important.

We have to learn to tolerate other people for us to be helpful to them and to ourselves. Every one of us was created to partner with each other so that we can better each other's lives. But without tolerance this purpose will be seemingly difficult to attain. The Apostle Paul puts it this way in his letter to the Ephesians.

"With all lowliness and meekness, with longsuffering, forbearing one another in love; 3 Endeavouring to keep the unity of the Spirit in the bond of peace." KJV (Ephesians 4Vs2-3)

We have to be meek and forbearing so as to help the other fellow relate freely with us. These are essential qualities that we all need to function successfully well in our day to day activities, especially where we have to relate with other people.

Your ability to train others in your skill demands tolerance. If you find it difficult to demonstrate this quality you will find it difficult to relate with others in your team especially those who are subordinate to you.

Every one of us has our various strength zone and weak zone, as we relate with other people. If you are hoping to add value to their lives there is need to do it knowing that we all do not have the same level of intelligence. If you can just give them a little patience you will latter find out that people will catch up quickly than when you are harsh towards them.

Personally, in my work with other people I have seen that a loving and calm atmosphere is a catalyst to learn easily than when people are put under unnecessary pressure. When people are going through a learning process, it is not the time to mount pressure on them because probably you want to make them know you are the leader of the team or their boss.

People will first learn how to do a thing carefully, before they will then become perfect and increase their speed in doing that thing. This is one area that most people especially leaders often fail to understand, they expect people to get perfect the very first time they do something as if it was that easy for them the first time.

People have different level of understanding, it's important to know that for some people you may need to explain more than once for them to get the message.

Those who do not tolerate others cannot train others in any sector of life.

One significant character or quality of a successful leader is the ability of the leader in question to develop people that could represent him in his absence. You must produce yourself among the people that you are leading in the team.

The question is this, how do you demonstrate tolerance to other people?

-Help them in areas of difficulties
-Respond to their questions if any
-Give encouragement to people
-Give the same instruction twice or more times if need be

Let us consider each of the above:

1. **Help them in areas of difficulties**

   A member of your team or somebody around you may be having difficulty in solving or addressing an issue that you felt he should easily handle for example, you have to give him a helping hand in resolving the issue rather than leave him there. It may not be much task, perhaps a little hand or a simple guide lines will solve the problem.

2. **Respond to their question if any**

   One simple way to show practically your level of tolerance towards people is the way you respond to their questions. The question may not be asked rightly or may not be irrelevant yet respond and place things in the appropriate way.

3. **Give encouragement to people**

   One way to help people grow well is to show them that you are concern about their success. Encourage them, even when they are doing below expectation give them hope, cheer them up. When you do this people will trust you and give more of their effort to please you.

4. **Give the same instruction twice or more times if need be.**

   In our dealing with others, especially in certain aspect of life where information or instructions need to be pass across.
   It requires us demonstrating tolerance towards those involved. Tolerance extends to your willingness to pass across the same instruction more than twice so that the person in question can catch every bit of the information.

ACTION POINTS AND WORKBOOK FOR CHAPTER TEN

The world is a place of interaction and like it or not our path will cross that of others either in the work place or other areas of life. For smooth human relation there is need for us to tolerate others.

Let us begin by asking ourselves these questions:

1. Have you been a tolerant people?
2. Have you being helpful to others in your approach to them?
3. From your experience do you think it is better when you are tolerant?

Here are the things to take note as we deal or interact with other people in the work place or other facet of life.

1. We are all from different background and this sometimes affects our behavior and performance.
2. The level of intelligence is different, so tolerate people by repeating yourself for proper understanding.
3. Encouraging people will help boost their moral and perform better.
4. Learn not to always be the bully type, but do so when it really calls for it to put people on the right track.
5. When people perform badly the first time, find it in your heart to give them another opportunity to learn to do it well.

Chapter Eleven

Be Realistic, Avoid Sentiment

Refusing to be realistic to yourself is one worst form of insubordination to self

Bringing out the best in you, demands being realistic and avoid sentiments. The greatest prison anyone can be is to be a prisoner of his conscience. Refusing to be realistic to yourself is one worst form of insubordination to self. The best thing you should always do to yourself is to tell yourself the truth irrespective of the circumstance.

One of the best things we should always do to ourselves is to be truthful to ourselves. Refusing to face reality or shying away from it is a worst form of creating self-limitation.

Today many people have become victim of not been realistic and this has most times become the root cause of failure in life. It's of no use to cover up the reality, because sooner or later the truth will definitely be known.

The big question is why are people not being realistic?

The reason or reasons for this is not far-fetched; see below:

-Lack of personal recognition

-Wrong view about life

-They do not value what they have

-Inferiority Complex

Lack of personal recognition

One of the values that we must always keep is our personal recognition. If you do not have value for who and what you are created to be then life is meaningless. In short, you have no reason to be amongst the living.

You should as a matter of pride and honor recognize that you are unique and special. You carry specific potentials in you and these cannot be found in another person. Until you recognize this firm truth life will not be fulfilling to you because you will always fill a sense of unsuccessfulness as a result of lack of personal recognition.

What keeps anyone strong and moving is the truth about his personality. If a man loses this identity he is forever doom into slaving himself to please others and to be like them and truly you cannot be like another person because you are created for a purpose and recognizing your personality is one strong factor that will make it a reality.

If you lack personal recognition, let me give you the best of advice. Rise up and be yourself regardless of whatever the situation might have been or is with you currently and you will see yourself becoming the very best that you are made to be. Let go this sentiment thing and face reality to make your life an invaluable one.

No one can make you less than your personality unless you create that yourself by the way you carry and present yourself before them. I always tell people not to look down on their person or on what they do for living, because there is much in you and that thing you are engaged. Others may not see it but there are so much to explore that will bring you to the best place that you desired if you can remain focused and determined in reaching your set goals in life.

Wrong view about life

Life is like a stage and we are created to act our parts conforming to the right standard and principles that will make life promising and satisfying. This cannot happen when you face life with a wrong mindset.

Wrong view about life is one factor that makes people not to be realistic. Some people see life as a competition, this misconception about life will force people to do things that are out of standard, breaking moral, civil and godly laws to be like others.

This is just quite unfortunate; they go through the pain and punishments when they are cut in these wrong acts. It's painful because they can easily achieve that same desire of theirs by simply following the principles that will make it happen and then wait for the right time for it to happen.

Some others feel life is unfair to them and so they take it on others by making things extremely difficult for others when it is in their position or power to handle issues regarding others. Most times these might have been as a result of the people they have interacted with in life who have fed them with wrong view about other people and they hold this view tight. It may also be as a result of the negative experience they had with people and so others will suffer for their past misfortune.

To be realistic is to face life with optimism, facing the truth not hiding under any misconception or sentimental influence that will affect your life, your career and others negatively.

Life is a give and take; it delivers back to you what you have given to it —quality and quantity. If your wrong view about it makes you treat others badly and you are a negative contributor to the difficulty that people go through, and you expect the best from life. You will have to change your view towards life first and treat people the same way you wish to be treated before you can see good things happen in your life.

Our life is a product of the sum of what we have done towards others and what goes around comes around. Be yourself; don't live a double standard kind of life. What is the benefit? If you are not satisfied with what you are delivering today, you can improve on it by changing your view about life and things and apply the best changes that will ultimately deliver to you the best tomorrow.

They do not value what they have

Each one of us is endowed with great talents and abilities that are perfect and distinguishing but what if someone decides not to value his? This is the problem with some people, they do not value what they have and so they cannot do anything with what they have.

Covetousness has made some people not to value what they have. They decide to go into some careers and professions that they do not have the talent for, leaving or ignoring what they can do well.

Take for example, an individual that has difficulty in mathematical and science inclined subjects going for engineering, when this person has some notable talents in arts and entertainment. This is like putting a square peg into a round hole, it won't fit in. It's a complete waste of time, effort and resources that would have yielded the individual a profitable result with ease and within a short time, if he has valued what he has and develop it effectively.

Inferiority Complex

Another area is to have inferiority complex, this character will make people feel and act below their personality and ability. People because they did not get higher education or because they came from a background that is not recognized and they allow these things limit them from exploring the opportunities they have to maximize what is in them.

All these factors can draw somebody behind but there can be positive change if anyone in such state is ready to follow the right steps to create new atmosphere of life.

Results of not being realistic

The resultant effect of not being realistic is completely negative; it makes an individual end up in woes and a defeated life. Let us consider some of these effects.

-Living in fear, afraid of being discovered

-Lack of trust among others

-Confusion as a result of false identity

-Inability to accomplish a meaningful goal or vision

-Cannot mentor others successfully

-Have no moral justification

I will briefly explain each of the above result of not being realistic.

Living in fear, afraid of being discovered

One of the effects of not being truthful to yourself and to others is fear. Fear is intimidating and whatever you are afraid of is what rules your life. This is a fear as a result of not living your real life.

Those who have claimed what and who they are not are always in fear when such issues are under discussion.

The conscience is an open wound; truth is the only medicine for it. Accept it or not the moment you hear or see anything relating to the false impression you have given about yourself there is a sense of quilt that creates emptiness in you. This is a dangerous state that can drive somebody to an early grave if it's not attended to as soon as possible.

Lack of trust among others

When you have something to hide, fear becomes your companion. You will become a loner, as a result of not wanting to expose yourself as you interact with others.

There is a sense of insecurity. Why? Because you cannot trust anyone. But quite unfortunate this do not last for long before people with this issue is been discovered. They either find out that they can't continue to pretend and deceive people and give up or they make a serious error that now exposes them into limelight.

Come to think of it why expose yourself, career and everything you represent to ridicule? In my opinion nothing on earth worth it. If you cannot live freely with others, it will be extremely difficult to manage it both in your personal and career life.

Confusion as a result of false identity

Whenever, someone gives or makes a false identity of himself, one thing is certain he has to continue in that same trend. What do I mean; he has to cover up that false identity with another falsehood. Immediately he has an idea that he is to be discovered, he will have to form another false to cover up that last falsehood. So the chain continues until a point the person is in confusion and cannot know which is which any more.

At this state the individual is like someone sitting on a timed bomb that will surely explode any moment. At this confused state nothing is clear; everything becomes complicated and sooner than later frustration sets in and the result can be very devastating and the truth is discovered.

Inability to accomplish a meaningful goal or vision

To be realistic requires a high standard of personal discipline, resolution and that will lead to accomplishing meaningful goals or vision in life.

If you are not realistic you will find it difficult to accomplish any meaningful goal in life. Goals or a vision represents us. This is the very reason we are living and must be in line with our real self. It is what we believe and willing to bring out everything in our real self to turn the dream to a reality.

If you are not been realistic, it will be impossible to get it done. Sentiment only lasts for a while; it cannot with stand time and the challenges that come with it.

Setting a goal may not be difficult for you but to get that goal accomplished is not realistic. This is simply because; you cannot be what you are not.

You cannot mentor others successfully

To mentor others successfully, means you must have a track record that is free from falsehood. The implication of this is that the person that refuses to face reality has no credibility to train, guide, and discipline others to a successful end.

You must be a person with clear record that has no character deformation that others will desire to imitate, to make their own life a beautiful and fulfilling one.

Have no moral justification

Moral justification is a strong value that only those who have nothing to hide can boldly declare in the open that they are free from accusing fingers.

Not being realistic in your dealings is a double standard lifestyle and one of the implications to this is that you have no moral right to query the wrong doings of others when you find them not worthy in any capacity.

This is one dread that is killing our society today, because most individuals have skeleton in their cardboard, it becomes extremely difficult to query the injustice, disorderliness that people exhibit with no sense of quilt.

This disease can only be eradicated if men and women will standup for justice and make the right changes in their individual lives.

A man who has something to hide cannot look at the faces of others without feeling quilt and pain of his deals. Think about it, it is self-defeat for you to get into what you definitely know that one day this same thing will drown you.

The best anyone can do for himself is to always face life being realistic to himself and to whatever he is engaged to. Sentiment most time last for a season and cannot be used as a base for us to live our lives.

ACTION POINTS AND WORKBOOK
FOR CHAPTER ELEVEN

One of the best things that can happen to anyone is to be himself. Until you face reality and cut off every form of deceptive sentiment you cannot accomplish yourself in whatever you have chosen to do.

The actions points to note are as follows:

1. Take a close and sincere analysis of your current life and discover if you are living your real self.
2. If you found out that there are areas you are not been realistic, make a change, a positive change.
3. If you live in your shadow you will not be able to explore the potentials inside you.
4. Life is lived more easily and there is a view of making it a meaningful one at the end of the day.
5. Be realistic to yourself, every man has a right to decide is own destiny and take responsibility of the outcome.
6. Be realistic to yourself by not following the crowd, you are created to be unique and to be original in all your life endeavors.
7. The only way to experience true joy and fulfillment in this world is to be practically true to yourself.

Chapter Twelve

Be careful and Rational in Decision Making

We are who, what and where we are today as a result of the decisions we made yesterday in life. Your destiny is a product of your decisions.

Life generally, is delicate, complex and complicated. However, life is very sweet, interesting and fascinating if you can only ensure extreme carefulness when it comes to making decisions. Living a carefree and adopting a careless attitude in making decisions is settling for defeat.

You cannot be the best with a careless or a carefree lifestyle. Every day in our lives we cannot avoid making decisions on issues of our lives –spiritual and physical.

Our life today is a product of the decisions we made yesterday. If you take a sincere look into every department of your life you will agree with me that the areas you are making progress are the areas you took better decision on and the areas that lack measureable progress are suffering as a result of bad decision.

One's ability to take the right decision in the specific time and at the appropriate place is a strategy that brings the best out of that person.

To bring out the best in us we must take this issue on decision with utmost seriousness, because this is what will make the very difference at the end of the day.

In this study on **"Be careful, Rational in Decision Making"** I will deal with some major topics that will help you get the best on this study. These topics are:

-**What are the areas to make decisions?**

-**What are possible influences on decision making?**

-**How can we make the best decisions in life?**

Each of this questions are of great importance and if they are well addressed in the life of an individual it will ultimately help in making the best of the individuals life –personal and career wise.

What are the areas to make decisions?

What are the areas to make decisions in life is a big and significant question. Decision determines destiny, our destiny lies in our hands. God has created us and has given us the model of life that will turn our lives purpose to a success.

If you go by the principles you will make the best of your life but if you go against the principles you have yourself to blame.

Decision making is a vital part of success in any endeavor of life, its one factor that determines failure or success. This is one thing that you have to do and ensure that you do it well. Certain aspect of life calls for someone to assist you in taking care of but when it comes to your life, I mean your life you are to take the decision after you must have had a good thought about the issue in question. None of us can afford to neglect this aspect of our lives; you cannot shift it to other people. If you do it yourself, you stand the chance of facing it squarely and seeing it to a success since there is no one to shift any blame to as most people do when things go wrong.

Let us see some examples of the decisions that we will definitely make in life.

-Our choice of lifestyle

-The academic level we desire to attain

-The choice of career we want to develop and build

-The place you dream to live

-The kind of personality you want to make your life partner

-The kind of financial stand you want to attain

-The kind of friendships you want to build

All these and more require good and lasting decision making, without which life will become very frustrating. I will briefly comment on each of the above areas that decision has to be made.

Our choice of lifestyle

Our lifestyles are of great importance if we are going to bring out the best in us in whatever career we find ourselves. The need to decide the lifestyle that will aid you in achieving your vision in life cannot be ruled out.

The lifestyle of a man is a driver to his destiny. If you resolve in your mind to make the best of your endeavor, then there are certain positive characters that you must maintain to make it a reality. It also calls for you to look out for and eliminate every negative character that does not go well with who and what you dream of becoming.

You must learn how to manage your time and every resource at your disposal to give you a maximum profit. Be diligent, determined and avoid any involvement that will not positively add value to your life.

You cannot live your life anyhow and expect the best of result. This is absolutely impossible. It is the life you sow that will determine the resultant harvest of your life.

The academic level we desire to attain

Academic level can play some good part in our life. You have to make a decision on the academic statue you want to have. It is not that everybody must obtain a high academic qualification but the point I want to make clear is that there are certain aspect or level that without a good academic training you may not operate in that area if that is what your vision is.

Today, there are so many opportunities to get yourself developed academic wise and if you do this it will go a long way to boost your life in all aspect. Ignorance is a drawback and can be very destructive at a high level. Read this:

"My people are destroyed because of lack of knowledge..." KJV (Hosea 4vs6)

You have to make a decision between getting knowledge and living in ignorance. Ignorance can be destructive in our current world.

The wise decision here is to improve your academic statue if you have the opportunity to do so. There is no doubt about what advantages awaits you if you are literate today more than the individual that is not educated.

The choice of career we want to develop and build

The decision of the kind of career you want to develop and build cannot be ignored if you want to make the best of your life.

Most people find themselves today in one career without an appropriate consideration if they have certain abilities or skills that will help develop and build an enduring life in that path.

Your career determines so many things in your life and if the decision is well taken it will be successful and fulfilling. Your choice of career determines your peace, joy, success, fulfillment and economic stand to a good extent.

If you fail in this area of your life then life will definitely become tedious and frustrating.

The place you dream to live

The decision on the part of the world you want to live should not be taken without understanding the place and know if the values in that part of the world will help you achieve your desired life or will hinder you.

Most people change from one place to the other based on sentiment or by trial and error hoping to be lucky and at the end of the day they have no remarkable success. You know why? You don't gamble with your life because you have only one life. There is no duplicate to your life and trying to mention luck makes you more vulnerable to destruction. Luck does not exist, we create what we call luck ourselves by our decisions, proper planning, development and positioning ourselves for the opportunity immediately it shows up.

There is a best in us and this best to an extent require the right location for a profitable manifestation. Don't move from one location to another location because your friends are moving without analyzing that place if you have a future in that place. If you do not consider it properly you may not see the pros and cons and what will definitely happen is that you will get stuck in life.

The kind of personality you want to make your life partner

One of the greatest and meticulous decisions that anyone must make is the decision of the kind of personality that will be your life partner.

Life partners will make or break you; it therefore requires carefulness to make this choice. If you make mistake in this sector of your life it will lead to a drawback in your life, both personal and professional endeavors will be negatively affected by this fault.

Partners are people that can help us reach our visions in life. How does this happen? We all have our strength and weak zones in life and with the right life partner we can complement each other's strength and weakness where necessary to achieve a successful life.

Think about it if the wrong choice is made then you are in for a troubled life. What makes two people to work hand in hand to a progressive end is agreement.

Without agreement no partnership can work successfully. Your life partner should be somebody that both of you have the same vision or common objectives in life and you Can easily agree together to move your lives to the next level.

Do you really want to make your life successful? Then don't jump into a life time relationship of marriage without a proper attention in the choice.

The kind of financial stand you want to attain

Financial decision is a must for all who desire something bigger than average. Desire is a powerful force that drives you to obtain what ordinarily you cannot by employing all necessary resources and potentials in you to make it a reality.

A good financial stand can do a lot of good to an individual; we all need money to accomplish so many things in life. If this is true we will have to plan and work towards accomplishing this. Read this:

"For wisdom is a defence and money is a defence ..." KJV (Ecclesiastes 7vs12)

"... but money answereth all things" KJV (Ecclesiastes 10 vs19)

The two passages of the Bible quotations are highly inspiring and this should challenge you regarding the kind of financial position you desire. Without a good financial stand you are like a man having hands but the hands are tied behind. I need it; you need it and everyone needs it. It's the instrument we use to acquire our economic needs in life, set our standard in life and much more it gives us the opportunity to help others who have needs.

A good decision regarding what your financial position should be like will be one of the best of decisions you will ever make and live to be joyful about. Good financial stand is a key to unlock the door to a beautiful economic life.

The kind of friendship you want to build

Every day in life we are sure to come across people. These people are of different ideologies, background and belief system. They can positively or negatively affect our lives depending on the choice of the friends we welcome into our lives.

Friends are to add values to our lives and help us achieve our purpose in life through their contribution to our lives. But if this is not seen then there is no need keeping that friendship.

This may be a hard decision to make but no need to be sympathetic or sentimental about this. You have to do what you have to do to move your life on a positive direction. Otherwise you will definitely waste the valuable part of your life on liabilities.

A good choice of friend will help challenge and motivate you towards pursuing and arriving at the shore of your dreams.

The decisions we make on the above areas that I touch are of necessity and this must be deeply considered to move your life to a better direction.

The seven (7) areas I choose are areas of life interests that almost everyone cannot ignore or run away from making decisions in their lives. Our decisions in these areas must not be handled with a carefree attitude but must be done with the purpose that this is what will determine how you will definitely arrive in life.

The next things that we will be considering are certain factors that possibly influence our lives and endeavors.

What are the possible influences on decision making?

The world is a place of influence, the people and the things around us that we are connected to, can directly or indirectly have certain influence on us. Some of these agents of influence include the following:

-Our family members

-Our friends

-Our Colleagues

-Our lifestyle

-Our environment

Let us see briefly how each of the above influences our decision making.

Our family members

We all belongs to one family or the other and somehow this family ties affect our decisions in life. The point here is that you should know what you intend to make out of your life and if their influence is going to negatively affect your life then there is no need to allow it.

As members of the same family they may be required to give their opinion on issues regarding some aspect of your life but when their opinion does not add value to you, wisdom demands that you should not subscribe to it.

Another important factor to note is the issue of sentiment on your part. It will be a great error for you to allow their negative opinion on you because of sentiment when the real truth is that it will lead you to a substandard life or worst still to destruction at the end of the day.

Our friends

The friends around us have both positive and negative influence on us. However, it's our duty to resist the negative influence and embrace the positive ideas and suggestions they give.

You must not allow friends to rule your life, don't get trapped with this friendship thing and you fail to understand that each one of us is responsible to ourselves and that includes taking decisions that will positively affect our lives now and the future.

The circumstance surrounding a friend when he made the decision he is offering as his own opinion to you might be different from yours now, so it requires you analyzing the different circumstances before yielding to the suggestion the friend is offering.

The summary is this, be open to the ideas and suggestions that each friend is ready to offer but never take a final decision on your issue until you have critically analyzed and be convinced that the decision you are taking will bring out the best of result at the end of the day.

Our colleagues

The personnel in the work place can also in some ways influence our decisions in life. Our colleagues may be very smart as regarding the job but that does not mean he or she will be smart when it comes to certain issues outside the job.

A colleague who is smart in the working field, but whose marriage failed as a result of his regular assault on the wife and children cannot give you the best of advice when it comes to marital challenge. Let us consider another example; a colleague who is a drunk and a traditional gambler cannot positively influence you when it comes to handling financial issue such as saving and investing.

If you consider the two scenarios I sighted above you will agree with me that there are certain colleagues that we must not go to for advice or suggestions seeing that they themselves are not doing well in that sector of life, otherwise they will lead us into the path of total destruction.

Our lifestyles

One of the strongest factors that influence the decision of a man is the lifestyle. We all have choice of lifestyle; some of us might decide to take the path of work, honor, integrity, godliness and contemptment which will finally results to success and fulfillment. Another person might decide to follow the path of dishonor, ungodliness and breakdown of moral and civil laws which of course will lead to woe and failure at the end of the day.

The two people above decide to choose different path of life, they do not think in the same direction and so to expect them to take the same decision on issues in their lives will be an error.

The way we live our lives influences our decisions, this is in relation to our mindset. It is this mentality that affects our decision making, if we have a positive lifestyle it influences us to take positive decision and a negative lifestyle will deliver a negative decision.

Our environment

Influence is a powerful force. You are either a victor or a victim when you come in contact with one. The environment you find yourself will try to influence you with her positive and negative factors. However, the wise and strong in mind will subscribe to the positive influence and object to the negative ones.

The fact that you live in an environment where people lazy about without a definite plan and purpose for their lives do not indicate a truth that you must be like them.

By your choice you can create the change that is expected in that environment but first the responsibility you have is to ensure that the negative structure of the environment does not affect you in your choice of making the very best of your life.

> ## Success is assured in the life of a man who refuses to allow his location or environment to influence his life negatively.

We have our choice to make; this is one beauty about life. Whatever we do not like in our lives we can change by changing the decision that brought us to that point in our live. With a better decision, things will definitely change for the best. No hope is lost as long as there is life you can still make the best of your life, it only requires one sincere decision in making the appropriate change that is required and you will see yourself moving to your next level of success.

Is this your desire then rise up, and take your place in destiny.

How can we make the best decisions in life?

How we can make the best of decision is the important issue that must be address carefully to avoid mistakes when we make decisions. The areas of focus on this topic will be as follows:

-Face reality, avoid being sentimental

-Think of the short and long term effects and benefits

-Be ready to pay the necessary price

-Random other peoples view regarding the issue in question

-Ask yourself the purpose of the decision

-Be open minded

Face reality, avoid being sentimental

In every issue that involves taking decision one thing we must do is to remain realistic and what we must avoid is being sentimental. When these two ends are achieved then the decision will be taken with the view of making the best of the situation.

To face reality is to be true to yourself. It's really quite unfortunate that some people will just take decision without being truthful. This is self-deception and will not take you anywhere forward because the real issue is yet to be addressed.

Take for instance, if you go to see a Doctor and decide to tell him that you have a stomach upset whereas your problem is a heart problem you are only deceiving yourself and not the Doctor. Whatever stomach treatment that is given to you will not change the state of your heart problem.

Until the real problem is addressed you will not see a lasting solution.

Think of the short and long term effects and benefits

Whenever we are making decisions in life there is need to consider the effects and benefits both short and long term.

Some decisions have a short term benefit but have a long term negative effect. Some decisions will give you a positive long term benefit. This is because it was a well targeted decision.

Life is not all about today. But living the best you can today to make the future a successful and fulfilling one will demand taking a decision that will have a long time benefit on you and others around you.

As we make decisions in life let us not be myopia about it but look out for the longtime benefits. This is one great and wise strategy we can employ and make a good decision in life.

Be ready to pay the necessary price

For every step of success in life there is a price to pay. The decision we will have to make in life may require a price to be paid.

For example, the desire to become a business owner is a giant step in life that requires you paying some uncommon price to turn that vision to a reality.

It's no child's play for anyone to have an objective to become a number one deliver of a specific product and service that will meet a world class standard.

It's a challenging decision to say you want to change your status in life to a higher, honorable and admirable one.

All these decisions are great but will not come so easy if you are not willing to paying the right price to make it happen.

It all requires great thoughts, strategic planning, resources determination, persistence, focus and actions to make it a reality.

Random sample other peoples view regarding the issue

Sometimes we may need to get more information on an issue before we finally take our decisions. In fact it is the best of steps to take in life when dealing with issues of life that demand decision. The question is why do we do this? This is because we do not know it all. We need others to contribute positively into our lives to bring us to the place of our best in life.

Life is a journey, and in this journey our path will cross with the path of others in this occasion we need to allow them impact our life with ideas and information that we need to arrive at the shores of our dream or otherwise receive ideas and information from them that we can employ now or someday to address issues in our lives.

These people may be older or younger than you, you may be more educated than them but the major point here is that if they have what you need to better your life as a result of their experience in such area do not hesitate in allowing them to mentor you. This is the very best you can do to yourself.

To ignore a source of knowledge is to accept ignorance with a great price of failure as the product.

-Uffoh Emmanuel O.

To be privilege to get other peoples opinion on an issue that you can carefully sample and analyze before addressing a situation is a great advantage on your part if you can do it well.

Most failures in the life of individuals are as a result of trying to run their life alone. To ignore a source of knowledge is to accept ignorance with a great price of failure as the product. There is no benefit in trying to do it alone when there are opportunities of human resources around you.

Ask yourself the very purpose of the decision

For every decision before us there is a specific reason or reason why it has to be, this reason or reasons must be understood without which you will miss the very fundamentals for the decision.

Whatever decision we are making today will go a long way in life with us and so it is highly important that the reason for the decision is not defeated.

I believe I have indeed extensively considered the topic **"Be careful, Rational in Decision Taking"** and the positive effect. We have also considered the negative effect if it is done wrongly. In summary if you are going to be successful or a failure in life it depends on your decision. The better decision you are able to make the easier you will succeed in your life career.

ACTION POINTS AND WORKBOOK
FOR CHAPTER TWELVE

To look before you leap will save you from ending up in the dish. When we exercise carefulness before we make decisions there is a possibility we will make the right decision.

1. Your life today is the product of the decisions you made yesterday. Take a sincere analysis of your life to confirm this.
2. Sit down and run through your life and find out if there are some decisions you took that has been negatively affecting you and take the right decision.
3. Life is not a static state but a dynamic process of step by step that requires decisions to be taken at each step to make it a better one.
4. Never take decisions when you are not in your best state of mind.
5. Learn to seek counsel from those higher that you before you finally decide on your decision.
6. We may have made a serious mistake in the decision we took some time in our live. Don't remain in the quilt and sorrow, correct it and move on with your life. Your future is far brighter than the past.
7. To take the best of decisions in life you must rule out sentiment. Never allow yourself to be influenced that you fail to realize your desire of becoming the best depends on your decision.

Chapter Thirteen

Show Mercy And Goodness To All

**To show mercy and goodness to others
is the access to real joy and prosperity.
What goes around comes around.**

-Uffoh Emmanuel O.

We all have dreams and aspirations that we desire to see come to reality someday if not yet attained. However, success does not come by default; it takes having a true vision, strong desire to bring it to pass, uncommon strategic planning, executing the plan and following through until the dream becomes a reality.

Now your set goal has become a reality, but is this the end of life? The answer may be yes for you and some others but for me it's not, and am aware that some people agree with me on this. What do you say about fulfillment? You wonder, Fulfillment is higher, a more noble attainment. This is a point where you touch the lives of other people as a result of your success.

We have a large number of successful people in the world today but a minute number of fulfilled individuals. Your life becomes more meaningful when you impact something good into the life of others.

To show goodness and mercy to others is a great value and this is the gratitude you offer to God as a result of your success.

As we journey through the path of life, our path will cross the path of others, ensure that the role you play in their lives will make them wish to meet with you again.

In the light of this, there are many questions that come to mind but three of them are of utmost importance.

-What is goodness and mercy?

-Why do we have to show goodness and mercy?

-How can we show goodness and mercy?

Let us briefly consider each of the above questions for clearer understanding.

What is goodness and mercy?

Goodness is a character of being good, showing a moral act to people that practical show your love towards them. Mercy is a state of compassion, forgiveness not paying evil for evil towards them who have hurt you. Mercy allows you to consider the state of people and that is what allows you to practically demonstrates goodness to them

These two qualities are not common virtues; it's only those with a godly heart that can make this happen to others. Showing goodness and mercy to others shows that you have a best in you that will not only be of interest to you but to others around you.

It's a common truth that we can't journey in life all alone, we need other people. What we make happen in people's life is what we can expect to happen in our life. As you show goodness and mercy to others it will someday pay off in your own life.

Why do we have to show goodness and mercy?

Some of the reasons why we should do this include the following:

-There is no encyclopedia for the self-centered

-It is a sowing that comes with great harvest

-It's the way to show gratitude to God

Let me explain these points briefly

No encyclopedia for the self-centered

The world has no encyclopedia for those who lived for themselves. Everyone desire to be remembered one way or the other, but this can only happen if we have lived a life that has positively impacted others.

The good things you make happen in the lives of others will leave your name in the book of record after you have gone. In our natural world we see men and women who have lived more than a century in books of record as a result of their deeds towards mankind. The question to you is what will you be remembered with? Is it the trouble and pain you caused others or for positive impact you made in their lives?

It is a sowing that comes with great harvest

The world is a field and everyone sow into it to make it what it is. Our harvest is a product of the type of seed and size that we sow into it. If you are sowing evil and mischief today, you will eventually reap misfortune sooner or later. There is no way you can escape it.

When people engage themselves in activities that work against others it is certain that one day they will find themselves reaping what they have sown. What goes around comes around, and the evil that men do, does not leave after them but follows them.

Read this:

"Even as I have seen, they that plow iniquity, and sow wickedness, reap the same." KJV (Job 4vs8)

On the other hand if you sow goodness and mercy in the life of people you will definitely reap the same good gesture in your harvest.

It is a way to show gratitude to God

One way to say thank you to God is to offer service to humanity. In every true and legal success, we put together some ingredients to bring it to pass, but mind you without the hand of God upon you things may not have worked out for your success.

The only way to show gratitude among many who tread the same path with you but are not able to come to the place of success is to touch the lives of others.

There are people who have better qualities you can think of. For example –skills, qualifications, connections, intelligence but somehow you are favored. This is why you owe God that service to bless the lives of others.

One of the worst forms of ignorance is for a creature to ignore his creator. It is like a branch that detaches itself from the main tree, it's only a matter of time it will dry and then die off. Never neglect this part in life, be ready to show others mercy and be a great source of joy to them if you are in the position to do this.

How can we show goodness and mercy?

There are various ways we can show or express goodness and mercy to others, some of these include:

-Through moral support

-**Material support**

-**Financial assistance**

-**Personal leverage**

-**Connection/network**

These are some of the ways we can show goodness and mercy to others. Let me elaborate more on the above.

Through moral support

In our world today you will agree with me that lots of people need moral support to keep them going. We can't afford to abandon people in their state of hopelessness and despondency. We need to come close to them and show them some love and encouragement.

Our moral concern and approach on people who are going through rough path in life can go a long way to strengthen and awake their self-consciousness that life can improve and become better than what it is now for them.

Material support

If you take a critical look around you will find that there are lots of people that need moral support. We can render this assistance; some of us have some wares and items that we don't have need for. We can give them out instead of letting it waste there in the store house.

There are people who are hungry, if you have more give out the extra. It is surprising that people will allow food items to get expire in their houses and there are people out there that need this food to survive. This is wickedness selfness in the highest order, have you ever heard of this:

"Give, and it shall be given unto you; good measure, pressed down, and shaken together, and running over, shall men give into your bosom. For with the same measure that ye mete withal it shall be measured to you again" KJV (Luke 6 vs38)

Whenever we give out we receive and it is amazing that what we receive is always better and more than what we gave out. If you have not tried it, it may sound strange. Give it a try and you will be more convinced about this principle practically than when somebody is telling you about it.

Through financial support

Achieved success most times comes with financial empowerment. In this regard you can decide to give out some percentage of your money to support others financially to help bring their visions or projects to a reality.

We can help in sponsoring those events or project that will better the lives of people in a community, state or country. You can give out scholarships; you can as well support people who need funds for medical attention. These are some vital areas that most of people neglect even with all their riches. Today, you can begin to make the difference in the lives of people all over the world if you can financially support the needy.

Through personal leverage

This is another way to show goodness to other people. Maybe you are skillful in certain field; you can give help to those who are still struggle in that area. Train people, organize lectures and tutorial that will help build their lives up in that career or field. Give out some of your products that people can use and get improved in the field or career you are connected with. If you can teach a man how to walk with his feet you would have saved yourself the work of carrying him on your back.

Connection/Networking

What some people need to keep going in life is connection to the right people and place. You may be the one that can help turn the lives of people around by this help. Are you influential or connected to the who knows who in the society? Use this to better the lives of others and you will be forever glad you played this role in their lives.

If this is what you have; you can contribute to the world by using your influence to boost the life and career of somebody.

In today's world, whatever we are engaged to we need to network with others for us to really succeed, so if you have a good network, why not introduce someone you know that needs it to make best of his life. The role you play in people's lives by leveraging them to their success Will never be forgotten. it brings joy and a sense of accomplishment to your life.

ACTION POINTS AND WORKBOOK
FOR CHAPTER THIRTEEN

People express goodness to others as a result of mercy. We should come to a point in our lives when we look out for people to show goodness to. Far and near there are people that require our goodness in their lives. Here are some ways we can show goodness to others.

1. Moral Support, There is one thing we can do to create positive impact in people's lives and that is to render moral assistance to them in the place of their needs.

2. Financial Assistance, We can show goodness to others by assisting them financially when we can afford it. You can change people's lives by contributing financially into their lives.

3. Personal Leverage, What do you do? You can train, mentor and bring others to success in that sector if you can personally take it upon yourself to leverage them.

4. Network, One of the fastest and easy ways to grow in life –personal, career, and business is by networking with others. Some of us have good networks that we can use to help others, see this as an opportunity to bless other people by connecting them to this network that will positively improve their lives.

Chapter Fourteen

Be Open To Change

Change brings challenge that gives birth to creative innovation that makes our world a dynamic one.

-Uffoh Emmanuel O.

We live in a dynamic world and every event and purpose experience this dynamism. You cannot bring out the best in you without complying with this principle of change.

One of the factors that make life more interesting and fascinating are the new creativities that manifests through these changes as a result of innovative mindset.

At least every six months there are remarkable changes created in many sectors and systems of the world. These changes come as a result of man's nature; the Economist said that human wants are insatiable.

We always think of creating changes that can turn the complexities of life into simpler form. This is where the best manifests. You cannot do a thing in the same way over and over again and expect a different result. In the same way you cannot run the same process or event using the same system and materials and expect a different result.

When we make the important and necessary changes in the right place and in the right time we also get the right result as the product. This is true in all sector of life –personal, career, business, employment, ministerial call etc.

Most businesses have become stagnated or even out of system because the people who are running it have refused to embrace the idea of change.

Change is the only constant phenomenon on the face of the earth. You are either creating the change or you are complying with a change that has been created. No one can stand neutral, it's not possible. You just fall in just the way water finds it's level.

There are areas of interest in this study, which we must pay attention to. These areas of interest include:

-Why do people reject change?

-What are the benefits of changes?

I will consider the above so as to give us a better understanding.

Why do people reject change?

Change is part of our world, its one constant factor that makes life challenging but interesting as well. Knowing the fact that changes are expected to come in one time or the other.

The question is why do people reject change? Let us look at some reasons.

-Fear of trying something new

-Self satisfaction

-They are shortsighted

-They do not want to invest more into the future

Let us look into each of the above factors why people reject change.

Fear of trying something new

People's perspectives about life are quite different and this is what we find coming to play in their general life.

Some prefer to stay on one thing and one method so long it's still working. They forgot about the three important elements that should be considered in whatever you do.

These three elements **time, quality and quantity** are so important. These are the yardstick to measure success in our life activities.

The individual who is rejecting change because of fear will not consider these factors. This is one of the things that cause limitation to progress in all facets of life.

If there are new systems that could afford you to improve on the **time of production, the quality and quantity of production** it is of huge benefit that you embrace that system. To stay in your old way of doing things is to remain limited and backward.

Self satisfaction

There is always a room for improvements in life. The day you say there is no more room for improvement is the day you erase your name from the future. The future belongs to those who believe they can transform the complexity of life needs today to simpler form tomorrow.

Some people do not welcome change as a result of this mindset of self-satisfaction. Don't get me wrong with the issue of contentment, I also agree with it. However, it's failure when there is room to move forward in life and you prefer to standstill.

With such mindset the individual or business will fade out because there is no room for such in the twenty first century.

Open your eye to the realities of life, change is a beautiful aspect of life. But this beauty can only be explored by those who create one or embrace the one that has been created by others.

If you see change as obstacle, it becomes one to you but if you see it as opportunity to explore what is in it then you can make the best of it. By giving it everything it requires to make the best of it.

They are shortsighted

What do I mean to be shortsighted? This is only being concern about today without a view of what level you want to belong or take your career and business to in the future.

If you only live for today without a thought and a plan for the future you are taking a dangerous risk.

Those who reject change only consider today, they do not look beyond the present. This is the reason they are often cut unware. If you consider some of the factors that have caused many stunted growth in people, one of them is the lack of insight for the future.

They reject the changes that come; unknown to them that this change is what will make them or their business to remain relevant in the future. If you are thinking of taking your life or life activity to the future you cannot become satisfied as a result of the present progress or success you are experiencing.

Looking beyond the present is one strategic formula that takes you to your future place in life.

They do not want to invest more into the future

For anyone or business to remain relevant at all time will require regular improvement that comes as a result of development and development comes with investment.

Refusing to make the expected change because you feel you will spend money is becoming an obstacle to yourself. When we invest on ourselves or into any venture we are actually bringing developing that comes with profitability at the end of the day.

You do not run things with the same old machinery and expect to catchup with others who have new improved machinery. They will be better off in time, quantity and quality of delivering their product and service to their clients. You and I know these are the expectation of clients -Faster production, good quality, quantity and good customer service.

Investing into your life or business is one sure way to experience ensure continuous success. This is wisdom that when applied will keep the business profitable at all times. Most individuals and companies are ahead of others because of this strategy.

What are the benefits of change?

Every good change comes with benefits attach to it and when we embrace the right change we benefit from it. For example some of the benefits of change include:

-It's a means to exploring other possibilities

-It brings new atmosphere and challenge

-Change is an eye opener and corrects errors

The above list will be looked into briefly to help us see how change is really a benefit.

It's a means to exploring other possibilities

One reason for change is to open other ways we can do something and get a better result in a lesser time. Every good change exposes to us other options and opportunities we can apply to improve our production level and/or improve the quality of our products and service.

It brings new atmosphere and challenge

Change creates a new atmosphere and challenges people to prove themselves. In life when we are used to doing a particular thing the same old method we get used to it. But the negative impact of this is that we feel that we are very good not realizing that we are far behind others who now apply the new method of doing the same thing.

Change in life -personal and career wise comes with challenge and it is this challenge that propels individual to do something about improving themselves to meet up with the current need of the environment they find themselves.

Change is an eye opener and correct errors

When we embrace or create change one of the things we discover is the error that is associated with the old system and find a solution to it. This is how we become the best. Those who are willing to welcome change will benefit from the change.

We don't become the best by living in the past; the best is current and fresh. This can be achieved by welcoming good changes.

ACTION POINTS AND WORKBOOK
FOR CHAPTER FORTEEN

Change is inevitable in our human life; it is a constant event in our world. Is either we are creating a change ourselves or we are accepting the created change. You cannot stand on the fence if you really want to make the best of your life and endeavor.

The questions are these what do we do with changes and are there benefits attached to change? Consider these helpful tips.

1. We are not to build a wall against change, but we have to welcome the change and then analyze it to see how it affects us.
2. Change most often brings new innovation; it is a phenomenon that increases productivity and good quality result in both personal and secular life.
3. Change helps us in discovering previous errors and drawbacks, so as to create a lasting improvement.
4. Change also comes with a price to pay to get that very best of the change. This is one factor that makes many not to accept change easily. They find it difficult to pay the required price.
5. One good benefit of every good change is that it helps to turn most complexities of life into simpler form. Thus making it more affordable.
6. Every change we are creating or decide to subscribe to should create or give positive impact in our lives and that of others ranging from personal, career, business, ministerial call, employment etc.
7. The principle of change is a powerful factor that gives us the power to turn things to our benefits in order to give us the best opportunities that life offers at any given time.

Chapter Fifteen

Keep Developing Yourself

The day you stop learning and developing yourself is the day you start depreciating

We are all special and unique personalities, created to accomplish excellent purposes in life. If you can understand this excellent truth and live in this premise, it will help you to pursue your life dreams believing their possibilities even when there are challenging issues that tends to truncate that dream.

This chapter and the rest in this book will center on certain personal human character and attitude that we need to develop so as to motivate and enhance our ability to bring out the best in us.

It is development that keeps anyone current in life. The day you stop learning and developing yourself is the day you start depreciating in life.

One way to make yourself valuable and relevant continuously to your world is to keep developing yourself in the things you do.

To live in the same old standard is to become outdated over a period of time.

In this twenty first century, we are witnessing new developments in different sectors of life –medical science, technology, food technology, pharmaceuticals, ministerial, academics, economy, information technology and government.

This makes the world more exposed and versatile. If you therefore remain in your old knowledge, it will make you stagnant. You can remain relevant and profitable to yourself and the world when you develop and improve yourself in your area of life endeavor.

How do we develop our self? Is the question that needs to be addressed?

How do you develop yourself?

There are various ways and avenues to develop ourselves today and some of them are as follows:

-Going for further study

-Be open to new innovations and ideas

-Partner with people who know more than you

-Set a reasonable standard for your life

-Be teachable; assume you know nothing

We will briefly look at these areas on how to develop our self.

Going for further study

One of the places to get training on the current changes is the educational environment. Through this further study we can acquire more knowledge and inspiration to face the future.

Taking a study or training in your area of interest in life will definitely improve your knowledge in what you already know and what is current as a result of change. This will open your eyes to updates and your performance in your vocation will positively be affected.

This step will no doubt give you an edge over the competing and contending atmosphere and factors around you.

Be open to new innovations and ideas

Stay open to changes and ideas, it does not hurt rather it helps you to improve. Information is important; having the right information is like having the right key to a door but if you lack the right information you will be stuck in life.

There is an error that I discovered in people that feel that they are talented in an area and so they believe that they do not need further training. Well it's a question of ignorance of the fact that there are always new innovations and ideas coming up and those who keep developing themselves will meet the necessary requirement of the present.

Read this word of inspiration from the Bible.

"The heart of him that hath understanding seeketh knowledge..."
KJV (Proverbs 15vs14)

It is the voice of understanding that makes you seek knowledge continually at all cost.

Partner with people who know more than you

In becoming the best you will grow from ground level to top level. This is a progressive step you cannot avoid and the best people you see today have gone through that journey.

Partner with people, I mean the best that have good track record will make your desire to become the best easier and faster in life.

Your partnership with those who are higher than you and have more development than you will create opportunities to develop and improve yourself. It is impossible to stay under a wise counsellor and remain foolish.

One useful advantages of partnering with others is that partnership create a platform you can use to exchange ideas and knowledge that will add useful information that will help elevate our life.

Set a reasonable standard for yourself

Setting a standard for yourself is setting a target to know where you want to be and who and what you desire to be over a set time frame.

The standard am talking about is telling yourself that you do not want to settle for average but your aspiration is to be among the excellent.

Be teachable; assume you know nothing

It takes a humble personality to be under a teacher. Without a teachable spirit you cannot be taught what you do not know. A filled container has no capacity to receive more unless it is emptied first.

If you don't empty yourself you cannot improve. If you are going to sharpen and add to your previous skills and knowledge, you will learn to calm down and be open to teachings.

Take a brief moment and question yourself if you need to keep developing yourself? Am convinced that you will deem it's highly necessary. One easy way to get outdated is to refuse to update yourself. I wish you will engage yourself with some of this means of development and improvement.

ACTION POINTS AND WORKBOOK
FOR CHAPTER FIRTEEN

One truth about bringing out the best in us is that we must always try to be ahead of others. The good way to do this is that we should continue to develop ourselves in the areas of our interest. Personal development keeps you current and relevant to your world.

In order to make this a reality in your life here are some action points that will help you analyze yourself and sincerely open to you the areas you will need to develop yourself.

1. The very first action to take is to take a sincere general audit of your life to find out how current you are.
2. You will need to fill out this form below, I call it "personal audit development form" (PADF) to help you find the area you need development.

Category	Need Development	Don't Need Development
Personal life -Physical Spiritual		
Career life		
Family life/ Relationship		
Educational Level		
Financial Management		
Human Relation		
Business Management		

You can extend the table as it suites your life issues, more important is to mark the empty row with the appropriate answer as in "Yes" or "No" where applicable to you.

3. I assumed you have gone through the point two above very sincerely? If that is true then the next point is to address the areas that you need to develop yourself to move your life to the next level.
4. Every step you take to improve and develop yourself is of great importance and will definitely pay off in a very big way.

Chapter Sixteen

Let Patience Guide Your Life

Talents, Skills, Determination, Self-belief are some factors to accomplish your vision but patience is needed all through the way.

-Uffoh Emmanuel O.

A life without patience is a troublesome one. In the journey of life, there are many issues that occupy and preoccupy people's life. These issues require actions and decisions to be taken.

In handling these situations, patience is required as we take actions and decisions so that we don't act wrongly. A singular wrong action or decision can cause an individual a whole life time to correct if at the end he is able to correct it.

In this issue of patience, two areas will be focused on.

-In what areas of life do we need to exercise patience? And

-How do we address impatience?

Let us look into these two areas of interest above.

In what areas of life do we need to exercise patience?

-When we are dealing or relating with people

-In your personal and career life

-When you have before you a short or long term decision to make

Let us consider the above for clearer understanding.

When we are dealing or relating with people

We need patience when we are relating with other people on personal or work issues. This is very important because we are all different, especially our mindset and attitude.

When we exercise patience when relating with people they are more relaxed and free with us. This condition will make them express themselves better than when they are tensed up because of our negative attitude towards them.

Most people have lost the possibility of being a help to other people because they do not show any form of patience in listening to their problem. If your daily activity has to do with you relating with people either through physical interaction or through any communication platform you must exercise patience for you to give them the best and also get the best from them.

In our personal and career life

In our personal and career life we may be confronted with a challenging situation, work or perhaps an issue that calls for our decision. In such state we need all the patience that we can get to handle the situation or make the right decision.

Be very sure you are in your best state of mind before addressing any conflicting issue or take a decision. This will save you from mistakes.

When you have before you a short or long term decision to make.

Examples:

-Career choice

-Life partner

-Business partners,

-Investment platform and

-Place to live

There are times we are faced with real life situations that we must make a choice. For example, the choice of life career, life partner and business partner. These are choices no one should handle lightly; you cannot afford to fail in these areas of your life. Life will become like living in hell and filled with woes. You must not allow yourself to be so pressed and you do any of this without allowing patience to take its natural course in you when doing it.

How do we address impatience?

Impatience is a dangerous character that has ruined many lives and career. A little act of impatience can cause a damage that cannot be amended. It becomes wise that we should exercise that little patience that is required to make that difference.

We can avoid impatience by employing these strategies.

-Do not be in haste in taking decisions / choice

-Do not be in haste in taking actions

- Patiently read through every document before signing

-Do not be too anxious on things

-Do not take life as a do or die affair

-Always take time to consider the pros and cons on every choice/ decision before acting

-Never take a decision or make a choice when you are in a bad state of mind

-If it is possible relate with a professional in the sector before proceeding to take your decision

These are key strategies you can apply and you can be sure that you will not fall short in your actions or decisions at the end of the day if you carefully put the above strategic factors into consideration.

ACTION POINTS AND WOOKBOOK
FOR CHAPTER SIXTEEN

Patience is a virtue that will help anyone in bringing out the best in him. It is one uncommon virtue in our world today and the lack of it has caused more harm than good to a lot of people.

Why do we need patience is the question to be addressed.

1. A life of impatience can be very destructive if not checked. Every day of our lives we will need to relate with others and often time's people do not speak or act as you thought they will do. It requires patience to relate with each person without hurting them or them hurting you.

2. Every day we will have to take decisions regarding our personal life or the life of other people there is need for us to do this with patience. Don't rush into taking decisions about yourself or others when you do not understand the issue properly

3. We cannot avoid the issue of choice making in life. choice ranging from career, marital partner, type of employment, where to live etc. all these and many more requires patience in other not to make mistakes that may not be reversed.

4. Life can be very fascinating but can also be rough. In such times when life becomes challenging how do we face it. Impatience can be destructive, so we need patience to carry us through the tunnels of life.

5. What do you do as an individual? Does your activity make you interact with others? Then you cannot do without patience.

Chapter Seventeen

Be Discipline

**A man without a disciplined lifestyle is a
man without character to preserve.**

You cannot bring out the best in you if you are not disciplined.
Discipline is a vital lifestyle to be the best in whatever you are
engaged in.

Discipline is the ability to control oneself without being compelled,
or forced to do so. It is one unique visible character of great men and
women.

To be disciplined means to condition your lifestyle in such a way that
your spirit, soul (mind) and body will act to conform to moral and
civil laws. This is one character that is rare among people, because
people are loose and find it difficult to control their emotions and
actions. We have to train and control our lives to conform to certain
conditions.

**What are some of the areas we need to discipline our self on? They
include the following:**

-Relationships (some friends you keep and those to eliminate)

-Mind your Desires

-The way you talk

-Time Management

-The places you go to

Let us have a brief look on each of the above areas that calls for discipline in our life if we are going to bring out the best in us.

Relationships (some friends to keep and those to eliminate)

Success or failure in life is a function of choice to a very great extent. The choice of relationships and friends we keep is one factor that can determine our success or failure. The friends you keep will tell us who and what you are and where you will possibly arrive in life because they are big influence to your life.

In this regard you need to be disciplined in this choice, don't be carried away by everyone that come around you. Some of those who claim that they are friends are in your life to rip you off, some to sell you out to those who want you destroyed. But there are friends that are even closer than a brother these are the people that discipline will help you to discover and keep them in your life.

Mind Your Desires

Let us consider the issue of desires –legitimate or illegitimate. There are certain desires that are legitimate desires and there are also others that are not. Yes, we are created to be desirous. The economist puts it this way that human wants are insatiable.

If you are on the way to becoming the best, you must check your desires; every time you allow yourself to be carried away by everything your eye sees, it will become covetousness. Your desire should be more of what will add value to your life or provide a progressive change in your life. I am proud to say that your desires should not be what will drag you backward or make you an embarrassment morally. Thus, your desires should be what will please God and He will grant you those desires. Let us see this quotation:

"Delight thy self also in the LORD; and he shall give thee the desires of thine heart" KJV (Psalms 37:4)

Sometimes many people desire a thing or a place in life because they saw people with such thing or they saw people who live there. Well, this is simply because people do not know what they really want in life; it is distraction to do things because you saw others doing it. You may be walking out of your divine purpose in life.

In our general world today, there is an endless list of people who are on their way to becoming the best but unfortunately lost out because of one or more of the desire they got themselves hooked to. There are so many things that have a way of distracting people's vision and keep them stagnant and frustrated in life. In short they are destiny destroyers.

Paul the Apostle, explained the need to control our desires, he mentioned that some desires may be lawful but they are not expedient. See the way it is stated in the Bible.

"All things are lawful for me, but all things are not expedient." KJV (1Corinthians 10:23)

The explanation is that all things may be seen alright and lawful, he cannot associate with them on the ground that they can cause more harm than good to anyone. If you desire becoming the best in any area of your life then you must separate yourself from any desire that will not add value or help you to attain that vision.

The way you talk

The way we talk is very important; often time's people have talked so much that they make themselves vulnerable for destruction. We should be careful what we say, the place we are saying it and to whom we are saying it to.

It takes discipline to control your tongue. If you can maintain quietness you will not easily sell out yourself or others around you through much talk.

Words are powerful; it can build up and can destroy also depending what you are saying, to who and the circumstance. I know that some people may claim that they are extrovert but that does not mean that your tongue should not be put under control. It is extremely important that you keep quite if you don't have something reasonable to say than to make a fool of yourself or say what will generate problem to you or to others.

Read some of these words of advice.

"Excellent speech becometh not a fool: much less do lying lips a prince." KJV (Proverbs 17vs 7)

The speech of a wise man brings healing to the wounded soul but a single word from a fool causes deep sorrow

Silence is not timidity or lack of words; it's building up inner strength and valuable words to say at the right time and the right place.

-Uffoh Emmanuel O.

Time Management

You cannot be thinking of bringing out the best in you and become generous with your time. Time is not a friend to anyone; you make good use of it to maximize your life. Let me put it in another way; you effectively use your time to profit your life.

Some of us are not discipline with our time, we procrastinate on valuable issues and responsibilities that should have help us achieve our desire to be successful.

On a very straight note if you are careless with your time you cannot be the best in whatever you are doing. It's a fundamental truth, take it or leave it. If you dare doubt me go ask a truly successful individual what time management has to do with becoming successful?

The important point here is that you should be much disciplined with your time to make the best of your life.

Let us look at this inspired word.

"To every thing there is a season, and a time to every purpose under the heaven: A time to be born, and a time to die; a time to plant, and a time to pluck up that which is planted; A time to kill, and a time to heal; a time to break down, and a time to build up; A time to weep, and a time to laugh; a time to mourn, and a time to dance; A time to cast away stones, and a time to gather stones together; a time to embrace, and a time to refrain from embracing; A time to get, and a time to lose; a time to keep, and a time to cast away; A time to rend, and a time to sew; a time to keep silence, and a time to speak; A time to love, and a time to hate; a time of war, and a time of peace" KJV(Ecclesiastes 3Vs1-8)

The above word of inspiration is packed with great wisdom for life. Your understanding of this great resource will determine your success or failure in life.

There is a defined time for every purpose in this world and accepting and working with this principle will add value and success to your entire life but refusing to live by this principle will bring you defeat, frustration and sorrow at the end.

One of the worst things that can happen to anyone is the inability to manage his time or to allow other people to run his time without any benefit.

It's only a productive use of your time that will give you an appreciable life, anything short of this will amount to nothing good. The summary of the above is that there is time for everything on the face of the earth. Set time for your life purpose and excel.

The places you go to

It's great to move around not being retarded in a spot. But we do not take this possibility for granted? What do I mean? There are some places that are just a lion den.

There are places we go to that gets us corrupt, exposes us to delicate people, put our integrity and career on the line.

It takes discipline to make the right choice not to go everywhere because your feet can carry you there. The aftermath effect may just be too regretting.

Benefits of a self-disciplined lifestyle

The life of a disciplined man is a life of result. He lives a lifestyle that yields him benefits. There are many benefits of a disciplined life but I will focus on three only. Discipline enables you to:

Manage your resource to a successful end

Every aspect of our lives involves managing resources; it's our ability to manage the resources available to us that assures our success in life.

One unique benefit of discipline is that the individual is able to manage the resources available to him to a successful end. Discipline is required for someone to take good custody of whatever that is put into the persons care.

The journey to becoming the best will involve the managing of resources –human, money, talents, ability etc. Without discipline one will not know the value of what has been committed into his hand and the result of this will be mismanagement.

It is possible to have all the human resources, money, talents and abilities to make something happen but without discipline you will blow up everything. This is one problem that has resulted to the failing of so many businesses and visions that people have done.

Discover and maximize talents and opportunities

In life what gets you success and eventually fulfillment is discovering yourself. This will put you on course of your purpose in life. But without discipline those talents and opportunities cannot be maximized to attain the set purpose.

It takes the combination of talent and opportunity to make things happen but discipline is what is needed to keep you on course until you arrive at your desired place of success.

Making the right choice in life

One of the factors that will definitely help us to make the best of our lives is the ability to make right and profitable choice. A discipline lifestyle is one key factor that will help us to do this; we are able to face reality considering what will be the effect of that choice on the short and long term.

The positive effect of a disciplined lifestyle cannot be over emphasis, without it you it will be difficult to come to the place of the best.

In my careful observation and study on becoming the best, I will boldly say that a disciplined lifestyle is one of the strong factors that will turn this dream to a reality.

ACTION POINTS AND WORKBOOK
FOR CHAPTER SEVENTEEN

Most people cannot bring out the best in them because of one major drawback call indiscipline. A lot of people are living a lifestyle that generates a negative influence on them and this go a long way to give a negative impact in their general endeavors in life. These action points will help in addressing such drawback.

1. You must check out the friends around you, there are some to keep and some to eliminate out of your life.
2. Consider your desires; some desires will rob you your birthright if not checked.
3. Our words are our bounds and words spoken are very powerful. The words you speak must be thought about before you speak. This is wisdom, for life.
4. You must be discipline with your time; time is an element that plays a vital role in our lives and must be well managed if you will ever become the best.
5. The places we go to is very important. Well, depending on the kind of personality you really want to be. Certain places will definitely put your reputation and integrity at risk.
6. Talents, abilities, opportunities are all factors that guarantees success in our lives but without a disciplined lifestyle each of these factors Will be amounting to nothing.
7. Every desired success requires discipline to make it happen but the lack of discipline will bring failure.

Chapter Eighteen

Be Diligent Towards All You Do

Diligent is a clear commitment towards your vision that leads you to turn it to reality.

Diligent means to be consistent, remaining steadfast and regular towards all you are engaged in -personal and professional life as the case may be.

In bringing out the best in you, diligent must be demonstrated. It is a common fact that challenges will face you in your activities in life but diligent is a resolution not to be stopped or hindered by the challenges or drawbacks that come your way.

To bring out the best in you in whatever you are doing, means perfection. Perfection is not a day job; you require a diligent attitude all through the way to become perfect.

Read these words of wisdom about the result of being diligent and adopt them into your life.

"Seest thou a man diligent in his business? he shall stand before kings; he shall not stand before mean men." KJV (Proverbs 22vs 29)

The above quotation is straight to the point; if you are diligent in your life interest, it will give you excellent result. With excellent result you single yourself out with a unique service or product. With this you stand before achievers and not mediocre. This is one of the benefits of being diligent in whatever you are engaged in doing.

A diligent lifestyle will bring riches to you. Read this:

"He becometh poor that dealeth with a slack hand: but the hand of the diligent maketh rich." (KJV Proverbs 10 vs 4)

Refusing to put your hands into action will tend to poverty. Work does not kill; it's the way of being productive with oneself that delivers success. The diligent hand will make riches.

A life of inconsistency will slow down the pace to success and will eventually retard a person's best from coming out.

The diligent person is always engaged in productive ventures, maximizing resources, skills, time and opportunities to make success. It is simply using everything at your disposal to achieve a desired success.

Let us consider another one.

"Wherefore, beloved, seeing that ye look for such things, be diligent that ye may be found of him in peace, without spot, and blameless." KJV (2Peter 3 vs 14)

Your desire to bring out the best in you is a great desire; everyone will look forward to achieving this. It means coming out spotless and blameless. However without a real character of diligent attaining this desire will be extremely narrow.

Diligent help you to create a standard for yourself and all those around you. Take for example; a business owner who maintains his timing of opening and delivering service, the customers will be more confident in dealing with him than other business owners who are not diligent in these areas of timing and delivering service.

One hallmark quality that all successful people have is their ability to be diligent towards the part of activity they have decided to pursue. It's a lifestyle that indicate that you belief in yourself and your chosen vision.

Whatever anyone is engaged in, if you are not diligent towards it you will never be successful in that venture. This is true because you will not give that venture your best; you lack the grip to make it a successful one. There is no commitment since you don't belief in the venture and making a success here is not assured.

In summary, diligent is a character that makes a man stands out from the crowd; it gives him a unique recognition and rewards him with honor and Excellency above his peers.

ACTION POINTS AND WOKBOOK
FOR CHAPTER EIGHTEEN

Diligent is the combination of commitment and consistency in life. It is a way of life that indicates you belief in yourself and in what you are engaged in. A diligent life gives light to life and stirs up something inside that motivates one to keep doing what he is doing to get the desired result.

1. Are you diligent to your decisions and your endeavor?
2. Can you look deep into your life and find out if you are diligent.
3. Get on track and allow diligent to guide your life.
4. A life of inconsistency will definitely reproduce an inconsistent result but diligent will give a more rewarding result.

Chapter Nineteen

Be Determined

Nothing is impossible to accomplish for a man with a determined mind

Determination is an enhancer in life that helps you to pursue your vision and succeed in whatever you do. It is a resolute decision that drives you to make a difference when it is not expected of you by others.

It is that power that motivates you to push forward, saying you won't give up on yourself or your dreams when everything around you is saying give it up! Let it go! You can't make it! It's impossible.

The character of determination is the difference between mere dreamers and accomplishers of dreams.

It is the inner potential that drives you to go the extra mile when others around you are giving it up and quitting in their place of destiny.

Determination motivates you to find a way to make the best of your life while others have conceded defeat based on the conditions and circumstances of things.

Success, prosperity, achievement and promotion in any sector of life are the dreams of all men but only few are able to turn this dream to reality. Why? Because it takes determination, the best in life comes as a result and matter of determination. Let me inspire you with this.

"Enter ye in at the strait gate: for wide is the gate, and broad is the way, that leadeth to destruction, and many there be which go in thereat: 14 Because strait is the gate, and narrow is the way, which leadeth unto life, and few there be that find it" KJV (Matthew 7vs13-14)

Read again the above quotation, and consider this statement below.

Bringing out the best in you is like entering the narrow gate, it takes determination to enter in and that is why there are many mediocre because they are not ready to pay the price of determination.

Determination is one character that separates and takes you to your place of achievement when others look down on you and say you can't achieve it. You are force to refuse what others think or feel about you. You move on believing in yourself and working extra mile to prove them wrong.

Are you almost giving up on your dreams of making your life a meaningful one? Don't do that, take a deep breathe and push on. A little input as a matter of determination will get you off the failure trail and take you to the place of success.

There are numerous personalities that have made impact in their place of callings but not without determination. Their achievements will not have been possible without determination. We can draw inspiration from these individuals.

Let us look at the life of few of these people and see how they can inspire us to success by being determined.

Examples of determination

Do you know that **Michael Jordan**, who is considered as one of the greatest basketball player, was not allowed to play in high school because his coach didn't think he was skillful enough? The world of basketball cannot be complete without the name Michael Jordan standing out in a gold.

What is the career you have chosen and you are almost backing out because of other people's opinion? Well, such challenges are inevitable in the journey to success. It's part of life but with determination you can overcome challenges and arrive at your desired success.

Most of us take **Albert Einstein's** name as synonymous with genius, but at his early age manifested certain challenges that others considered him as a good for nothing child. Einstein had the problem of speaking until he was four and reading was another problem until he was seven. The teachers and parents thought of him as mentally handicapped. Albert Einstein was also expelled from school. He was refused admittance to the Zurich Polytechnic School. Well, it took him some time but when he took off he did brilliantly well and won Nobel Prize and of course changing the modern day physics.

Oprah Winfrey, she is one of the most iconic faces on TV as well as one of the richest and most successful women in the world. Oprah faced difficult times in her journey to this hallmark position. She was abused as a child as well as numerous career setbacks including being fired from her job as a television reporter because she was considered not suitable. But with determination she has become who and what she is today. This is determination.

Thomas Edison, This is another personality who became something as a result of determination. Edison's teacher said he was "too stupid to learn anything." at his early years. He wasn't better in the work place; he was fired from his first two jobs as a matter of not being productive enough. Even as an inventor, Edison made 1,000 attempts at inventing the light bulb. Of course, all those unsuccessful attempts finally resulted in the design that worked. The Electric Bulb.

Determination is a strong will to make it happen, to dispute the misconceptions that people hold towards you and your vision. All these men and women made remarkable impact in their various worlds as a matter of determination. You too can set the pace today in becoming the best in your place of calling. What it requires is a determination to make a difference.

ACTION POINTS AND WORKBOOK
FOR CHAPTER NINETEEN

You require determination to set the pace in whatever you are called to do especially when you are seen as unfit in the first place. But nothing is impossible with the man with a determination to make the difference and to prove others wrong.

1. First, you must settle in your mind that you will become the best at the end of the day.
2. You must be ready to pay all required price on your part to make that desire a reality.
3. Self-belief is a must if your determination will work.
4. Be ready to erase other people's opinion about you and what you intend to do.
5. Don't forget that you need patient and focus all through the way as you remain determined.

Chapter Twenty

Seek For Opportunities To Prove Your Self

**Opportunities are keys to unlock your
door of success in whatever you do.**

*"To every thing there is a season, and a time to every purpose
under the heaven: 2 A time to be born, and a time to die; a time
to plant, and a time to pluck up that which is planted; 3 A time to
kill, and a time to heal; a time to break down, and a time to build
up" (KJV Ecclesiastics 3 vs 1 – 3)*

*"I returned, and saw under the sun, that the race is not to the
swift, nor the battle to the strong, neither yet bread to the wise, nor
yet riches to men of understanding, nor yet favour to men of skill;
but time and chance happeneth to them all." (KJV Ecclesiastics 9
vs 11)*

The two quotations above open to us the realities that time and chance
(opportunities) are two factors that can help you bring out the best in
you. Most importantly, we see the express declaration that everything
has it's time and season. We go for opportunity in the right time
otherwise it will be missed.

If you will definitely become successful in life by bringing out the
best in you there is need to first make the due preparations. The
preparations to make are to set your mind for a purpose, develop your
talents and abilities in the right time and then focus in the direction of
likely opportunities.

Opportunity is a thing of the mind and eyes; if the mind does not imagine and hunger for it, the eyes does not look out for it. Where other people see drawbacks and obstacles the man who is looking for the right opportunity will see one and key into it to make the best of his life.

I will show you an example of opportunity in the Bible it's a long passage but take your time and digest it, this will help you draw out the inspiration within it. This is the story of David and Goliath, an amazing one indeed.

1 Now the Philistines gathered together their armies to battle, and were gathered together at Shochoh, which belongeth to Judah, and pitched between Shochoh and Azekah, in Ephes–dammim. 2 And Saul and the men of Israel were gathered together, and pitched by the valley of Elah, and set the battle in array against the Philistines. 3 And the Philistines stood on a mountain on the one side, and Israel stood on a mountain on the other side: and there was a valley between them. 4 And there went out a champion out of the camp of the Philistines, named Goliath, of Gath, whose height was six cubits and a span. 5 And he had an helmet of brass upon his head, and he was armed with a coat of mail; and the weight of the coat was five thousand shekels of brass. 6 And he had greaves of brass upon his legs and a target of brass between his shoulders. 7 And the staff of his spear was like a weaver's beam; and his spear's head weighed six hundred shekels of iron: and one bearing a shield went before him. 8 And he stood and cried unto the armies of Israel, and said unto them, Why are ye come out to set your battle in array? am not I a Philistine, and ye servants to Saul? choose you a man for you, and let him come down to me. 9 If he be able to fight with me, and to kill me, then will we be your servants: but if I prevail against him, and kill him, then shall ye be our servants, and serve us. 10 And the Philistine said, I defy the armies of Israel this day; give me a man, that we may fight together. 11 When Saul and all Israel heard those words of the Philistine, they were dismayed, and greatly afraid. 12 Now David was the son of that Ephrathite of Beth–lehem–judah, whose name was Jesse; and he had eight sons: and the man went among men for an old man in the days of Saul. 13 And the three eldest sons of Jesse went and followed Saul to the battle: and the names of his three sons that went to the battle were Eliab the firstborn, and next unto him Abinadab, and the third Shammah. 14 And David was the youngest: and the three eldest followed Saul. 15 But David went and returned from Saul to feed his father's sheep at Beth–lehem. 16 And the Philistine drew near morning and evening, and presented himself forty days. 17 And Jesse said unto David his son, Take now for thy brethren an ephah of this parched corn, and these ten loaves, and run to the camp to thy brethren; 18 And carry these ten cheeses unto the captain of their thousand, and look how thy brethren fare, and take their pledge. 19 Now Saul, and they, and all the men of Israel, were in the valley of Elah, fighting with the Philistines. 20 And David rose up early in the morning, and left the sheep with a keeper, and took, and went, as Jesse had commanded him; and he came to the trench, as the host was going forth to the fight, and shouted for the battle. 21 For Israel and the Philistines had put the battle in array, army against army. 22 And David left his carriage in the hand of the keeper of the carriage, and ran into the army, and came and saluted his brethren. 23 And as he talked with them, behold, there came up the champion, the Philistine of Gath, Goliath by name, out of the armies of the Philistines, and spake according to the same words: and David heard them. 24 And all the men of Israel, when they saw the man, fled from him, and were sore afraid. 25 And the men of Israel said, Have ye seen this man that is come up? surely to defy Israel is he come up: and it shall be, that the man who killeth him, the king will enrich him with great riches, and will give him his daughter, and make his father's house free in Israel. 26 And David spake to the men that stood by him, saying, What shall be done to the man that killeth this Philistine, and taketh away the reproach from Israel? for who is this uncircumcised Philistine, that he should defy the armies of the living God? 27 And the people answered him after this manner, saying, So shall it be done to the man that killeth him. 28 And Eliab his eldest brother heard when he spake unto the men; and Eliab's anger was kindled against David, and he said, Why camest thou down hither? and with whom hast thou left those few sheep in the wilderness? I know thy pride, and the naughtiness of thine heart; for thou art come down that thou mightest see the battle. 29 And David said, What have I now done? Is there not a cause? 30 And he turned from him toward another, and spake after the same manner: and the people answered him again after the former manner. 31 And when the words were heard which David spake, they rehearsed them before Saul: and he sent for him. 32 And David said to Saul, Let no man's heart fail because of him; thy servant will go and fight with this Philistine. 33 And Saul said to David, Thou art not able to go against this Philistine to fight with him: for thou art but a youth, and he a man of war from his youth. 34 And David said unto Saul, Thy servant kept his father's sheep, and there came a lion, and a bear, and took a lamb out of the flock: 35 And I went out after him, and smote him, and delivered it out of his mouth: and when he arose against me, I caught him by his beard, and smote him, and slew him. 36 Thy servant slew both the lion and the bear: and this uncircumcised Philistine shall be as one of them, seeing he hath defied the armies of the living God. 37 David said moreover, The LORD that delivered me out of the paw of the lion, and out of the paw of the bear, he will deliver me out of the hand of this Philistine. And Saul said unto David, Go, and the LORD be with thee. 38 And Saul armed David with his armour, and he put an helmet of brass upon his head; also he armed him with a coat of mail. 39 And David girded his sword upon his armour, and he assayed to go; for he had not proved it. And David said unto Saul, I cannot go with these; for I have not proved them. And David put them off him. 40 And he took his staff in his hand, and chose him five smooth stones out of the brook, and put them in a shepherd's bag which he had, even in a scrip; and his sling was in his hand: and he drew near to the Philistine. 41 And the Philistine came on and drew near unto David; and the man that bare the shield went before him. 42 And when the Philistine looked about, and saw David, he disdained him: for he was but a youth, and ruddy, and of a fair countenance. 43 And the Philistine said unto David, Am I a dog, that thou comest to me with staves? And the Philistine cursed David by his gods. 44 And the Philistine said to David, Come to me, and I will give thy flesh unto the fowls of the air, and to the beasts of the field. 45 Then said David to the Philistine, Thou comest to me with a sword, and with a spear, and with a shield: but I come to thee in the name of the LORD of hosts, the God of the armies of Israel, whom thou hast defied. 46 This day will the LORD deliver thee into mine hand; and I will smite thee, and take thine head from thee; and I will give the carcases of the host of the Philistines this day unto the fowls of the air, and to the wild beasts of the earth; that all the earth may know that there is a God in Israel. 47 And all this assembly shall know that the LORD saveth not with sword and spear: for the battle is the LORD'S, and he will give you into our hands. 48 And it came to pass, when the Philistine arose, and came and drew nigh to meet David, that David hasted, and ran toward the army to meet the Philistine. 49 And David put his hand in his bag, and took thence a stone, and slang it, and smote the Philistine in his forehead, that the stone sunk into his forehead; and he fell upon his face to the earth. 50 So David prevailed over the Philistine with a sling and with a stone, and smote the Philistine, and slew him; but there was no sword in the hand of David. 51 Therefore David ran, and stood upon the Philistine, and took his sword, and drew it out of the sheath thereof, and slew him, and cut off his head therewith. And when the Philistines saw their champion was dead, they fled. 52 And the men of Israel and of Judah arose, and shouted, and pursued the Philistines, until thou come to the valley, and to the gates of Ekron. And the wounded of the Philistines fell down by the way to Shaaraim, even unto Gath, and unto Ekron. 53 And the children of Israel returned from chasing after the Philistines, and they spoiled their tents. 54 And David took the head of the Philistine, and brought it to Jerusalem; but he put his armour in his tent. 55 And when Saul saw David go forth against the Philistine, he said unto Abner, the captain of the host, Abner, whose son is this youth? And Abner said, As thy soul liveth, O king, I cannot tell. 56 And the king said, Enquire thou whose son the stripling is. 57 And as David returned from the slaughter of the Philistine, Abner took him, and brought him before Saul with the head of the Philistine in his hand. 58 And Saul said to him, Whose son art thou, thou young man? And David answered, I am the son of thy servant Jesse the Beth–lehemite. KJV (1 Samuel 17vs1-end)

Now the important inspirations from this passage with respect to opportunity are these:

-David has already discovered himself as skillful in facing challenge.

-He was prepared for such opportunity.

-He was able to recognize that this is an opportunity to bring out the best in him because his eyes and mind were tune towards it.

-David refused to allow anyone to intimidate or deny him this opportunity by being determined.

Preparation and readiness are another connecting links to seeing and securing lasting opportunities in life. Opportunity or opportunities does not walk up to you so cheap, but it comes most times in disguise. What it means is that you need to pay the required price to secure it.

In today's world nobody sits and wait for the opportunity to come to them rather people that really desire being the best in what they do move towards the directions where opportunities are suspected to be available.

How does this happen?

Each day we wake up the same quantity and quality of time is deposited into our hands irrespective of our background, location and status. The desire to make your life a meaningful one is one of the motivating factors that propel you to move out and connect with people and places where you will possibly find opportunity to sell and prove yourself in your area of interest.

One great truth that must be registered in your heart or mind is that every day, there are different great and employable opportunities flying everywhere around us. The secret is this, opportunity is not noisy, and it does not standstill like a signpost that is always static at one point. Opportunity comes gently and once you do not recognize and use it to your benefit it moves on until another person sees it and uses it.

Another important characteristic of opportunity is that most often it does not come on a platter of gold; it always comes with some difficulties attached to it but the wise and those hungering to make the best of their lives will not allow these obstacles or barriers to turn them away from exploring the opportunity and maximizing the possibilities attached to that opportunity.

Can I ask you a question? Have you ever missed opportunity? Am sure that you felt so bad, when you latter discovered that the situation that was considered a problem was supposed to be your greatest opportunity to accomplish your life vision.

In summary, you can't make the best of your life if you are not looking out for the right and timely occasion to exhibit what you have in you.

The secret is this, in every location you find yourself home or abroad look out for something that you can do or use to prove yourself. Secondly, as we connect or network with people understand that there are great opportunities in that meeting listen carefully and watch closely and you will be surprise of the great and numerous opportunities to explore within those situations that looks like a barrier.

ACTION POINTS AND WORKBOOK
FOR CHAPTER TWENTY

Each one of us needs opportunity in one place or the other to be able to actualize our desired purpose in life. Opportunities are privileges or platforms given to us to prove our abilities and whatever we can do.

1. You must be prepared first in advance to be able to maximize opportunity when it comes.

2. Seeking for opportunity? You must set your mind and eyes watching out for the possibility of one wherever you find yourself.

3. Successful people do not wait for opportunity to come to them but they network with people and move towards the path that they suspect that opportunity can be discovered.

4. Sit down and do a good strategic planning and preparation towards your next expected opportunity, so that you don't miss it.

5. Never underrate or undervalue any privilege that comes to you, this may be a little beginning but that will definitely lead to a great result.

6. Every time you have a privilege or platform to showcase your talents, skills or abilities never joke with it, maximize it for you may never have such opportunity again.

7. Wherever you find yourself, you cannot be stranded if you can take your time to understand the environment and see the opportunities you can explore to make best of your life.

Chapter Twenty One

Be Passionate In Whatever You Do

Passion is a lubricant that drives you through every friction in the journey to your place of becoming the best. –Uffoh Emmanuel O.

"Whatsoever thy hand findeth to do, do it with thy might; for there is no work, nor device, nor knowledge, nor wisdom, in the grave, whither thou goest." (KJV Ecclesiastes 9vs10)

Passion is obviously one important quality that I will boldly say will guarantee your success; this is one element that will inspire you to do something – joyfully, meaningfully, effectively and efficiently.

Passion is what it takes to do whatever you are doing with joy and ease. Whatever we are engaged in doing we need a passionate mindset to make the very best of that endeavor.

To bring out the best in you, you must develop absolute passion towards your work or activity. It is absolutely a life of deception to get yourself doing what you have no passion for.

Trying to engage yourself in what you see others doing without passion for it is a waste of time. It's only a question of time, when the tough times and challenges begins to unfold in your track of activity, there is no assurance that you will not back out. The only sure power or weapon to conquer in such times is your passion for that which you are engaged in.

Most often people get into what they see others do or they are just hoping to get some break in life, in regard to financial upgrade, or to derive some social recognition. Quite unfortunate this is a wrong approach towards making life a meaningful one. The motivating element or factor here is not passion and so there is no enthusiasm to really carry on with this activity if for example the anticipated money does not start flowing in immediately. This is the reason why most business fails within six months to one year of operation. The same reason you see people changing careers overtime, simply because they never had a passion for it before they jumped into it.

Passion is a motivational element; it's a strong positive drive that comes from the inner man creating first a belief system in yourself that you have something good to offer or deliver that will definitely be a need to others. It is this conviction and motivation that keeps you from quitting until you arrive at the shores of your success.

Passion is an encouraging factor in the journey of life. Whatever area of activity we are engaged in, call it secular or spiritual; there are discouraging elements, factors including man that will almost force you out of your chosen endeavor but what gives you the courage to stay on it until you make things happen as you expect it to be is passion for that endeavor.

Getting yourself up, your business or whatever career you have choose demand first self-belief, a convicting self-confidence, determination and passion. With these qualities you can stand up and face your vision to a successful end.

Passion and diligent are linked together. Everything about life is all about getting positive result at the end of whatever you are engaged in. It is the belief that your life and career has a promising future that creates this passion for it and makes you do it being diligent all through.

The question is this, what are you passionate about? It is doing what you are passionate about that guarantees you being the best. If you miss this then you cannot bring out the best in you because your best is in your place of passion.

One of the elements or factor that stops people from getting things done is fear. It is false experiences appearing real. What fear does is to create lack of belief. It forces and intimidates people to accept negative perceptions. Fear comes in different forms and affects people in all works of life. One of the factors that can give people edge over fear is the passion they have for that particular career or activity.

It is this passion that strengthens you and makes you conquer the force of fear that forces people to stop fighting and concede to fear. If you have the passion for your choice of endeavor you will definitely make it to the top, it's only a question of time and patience and keep doing your best and you will see your expectation coming to reality.

ACTION POINT AND WORKBOOK
FOR CHAPTER TWENTY ONE

Becoming the best in any endeavor you intend to pursue in life demand passion. Passion is the burning desire about a thing or an endeavor that keeps you strongly attached to it until your whole being is totally consumed to it.

1. Passion is expressing an uncommon affection in your activity, so be passionate about your work.
2. Passion drives you to keeping doing the work even when the expected reward is yet to come.
3. Passion gives you strength to keep on in the midst of discouraging factors.
4. Passion is finding joy and fulfillment in your work.
5. Passion is what encourages you to go the extra mile that others are not ready to go to make it to the best.

Final Word

I believe you have read every page of this book and you have seen clearly that each one of us is created with all we need to function and become the best in our areas of choice in life.

This is one truth you must believe and live with before taking the next step, which is living your life according to the principles revealed in this book.

If you will become the best after reading this book depends on you, yes you are the architect of your failure or success in life based on three factors **-your mindset; believe system and your lifestyle.** Taking the necessary action required of you is often what separates the best from the common. Life is a journey; every journey constitutes ups and downs, it's our ultimate responsibility to maintain a forward dynamic pace that will take us to the place of the best.

This book is structured in a simple and systematic manner that anyone can understand and work with to take his life to the very place of success.

This book **"BRINGING OUT THE BEST IN YOU"** is unique and written with an ultimate objective to bring self-discovery and accomplishment in people's life. It will help you change every misconception, low self-mentality, a mindset of impossibility and create a positive atmosphere around you that will walk you into a lifestyle that will help you become the best.

The information in this book is the key to unlock the door of outstanding progress, joy and peace for an enduring life to anyone.

You have received the key information in making yourself the best through this book.

I am greatly excited to have delivered this work and hope that as you apply these principles you will become your expectation.

Printed in the United States
By Bookmasters